12/25/23

Merry Christmas to
Will & Cody

Love, Grandpa Michael
& Grandma Stephi

NOEL FITZPATRICK

Illustrated by Emily Fox

THE SUPER PETS

and ME

wren
&rook

First published in Great Britain in 2023 by Wren & Rook

ISBN: 978 1 5263 6462 3
Exclusive Signed Edition: 978 1 5263 6656 6

1 3 5 7 9 10 8 6 4 2

Wren & Rook
An imprint of
Hachette Children's Group
Part of Hodder & Stoughton
Carmelite House
50 Victoria Embankment
London EC4Y 0DZ

An Hachette UK Company
www.hachette.co.uk
www.hachettechildrens.co.uk

Printed and bound in Great Britain by Clays Ltd, Elcograf S.p.A.

May everyone who I am lucky enough
to reach with this little book be filled with
unconditional compassion and curiosity for
the wellbeing of all living creatures,
animal and human.

We *can* change the world for the better,
if we seek a way to understand and love each
other more, one 'humanimal' at a time!

CONTENTS

INTRODUCTION

A question I'm asked a great deal by young people is, 'When did you decide to become a vet?'

They think there must have been an exact moment when inspiration struck and my life's path changed forever. And although I can sort of point to such a thunderbolt, I think I was always destined to end up in animal care.

Animals have been a part of my life since before I could talk or walk. I grew up with creatures large and small on a farm, and since then I've treated thousands that come through the doors of my veterinary practice. I've had dozens of **animal companions** in my fifty-and-a bit years, and each one has taught me something. Some of the lessons have been minor, others I'll never forget.

It's not an exaggeration to say that without them all, I wouldn't be the person I am today. **You might know me from my TV show, which is called *The Supervet*, but filming that is only a small part of my life.** I work every single day at my veterinary practice, with a huge team of dedicated and caring colleagues. I'm a specialist in what's called **'neuro—orthopaedic surgery'**, which means cutting open and operating on patients to fix problems with the skeleton, muscles, tendons, spine and nerves. Sometimes these operations can be very complicated and take many hours.

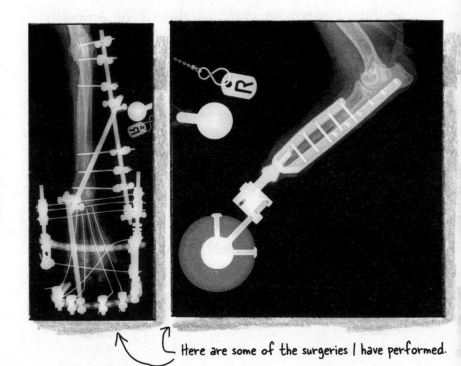

Here are some of the surgeries I have performed.

I'm especially known for 'bionic surgery', which means attaching and inserting man-made body parts, including implants and prostheses, to fix our patients' problems. I often design them myself alongside a team of engineers, so that I can tailor them to meet the specific needs of the animal I'm trying to help. For all of the so-called 'bionic surgeries' I perform, I believe that 'simple is best', and that if there is a simple solution to a problem, we should always use that.

People sometimes think that any implant in a human or animal body is bionic, for example a plate and screws or pins and cement to repair a fracture. But this isn't really true – it's just an implant used to help get your body working as near to normal as possible again.

On the other hand, when I said 'bionic', did you instantly think of a robotic animal with super-animal powers? I bet most readers of this book thought so and there is a good reason for that.

The word was actually made up by an American doctor called Jack E. Steele in the 1950s when he mashed two words together – biology and electronics. It then became a really popular term in the 1970s when two TV programmes, *The Six*

Million Dollar Man and *The Bionic Woman*, shot to fame. I loved the show *The Six Million Dollar Man*. It was about a guy who was very badly injured in a plane crash and who had two legs, one arm and one eye replaced with electromechanical implants. This gave him great strength and allowed him to run faster and to see things normal humans couldn't. After the success of the TV show, the term 'bionic' was often used to refer to someone with superhuman powers or with electronic or mechanical parts attached to them. With modern technology, such things *are* becoming possible, but we're still some way off a real 'Six Million Dollar Man'.

Instead, some of the animals I work with truly are bionic! Often, they come to see me because **parts of their bodies are missing**. This might be because they were born that way or have had an accident, or because the body part needed to be

removed due to a disease such as cancer. So, my team and I invent devices that do just what that body parts would do, and implant them into the animal so their body can function again. They don't give my patients superpowers. But as you will soon find out, many of my inventions have been inspired by superheroes that I've read about in **comic books**.

The word 'Supervet' suggests I have all the answers. And with modern technology, hard work and love, I *can* fix many problems. But not all the time. Sometimes the problems can be impossible to solve and I fail. Sometimes I end up recommending that we remove an entire limb, which is called **an amputation**, or sadly a patient is allowed to pass peacefully away, which we call **euthanasia**. Each day I try to learn and be better. I hope this book will give you a 'warts-and-all' picture of my life – the challenges, the failures and the successes. One thing's for sure: every single new idea I've ever had to solve a problem came from what I learned from past failures. Every time I get something right, it's because either myself or someone else got it wrong before.

This book is going to cover my journey through life, from a young boy with big dreams of caring for animals and getting them out of pain, to where I am today, with more than a hundred colleagues in our large vet practice, still looking for a way to make my dream a reality. If I were to boil down my dream to one single statement, it would be that I want to give our companion animals a 'fair deal'. **Animals give us so much love.** We should give them everything we can back. My dream is for animals to have access to the very best healthcare, to feel loved and to be protected.

If I'm going to succeed with my dream, I need to convince all of you to help me.

And you can. Your generation gives me hope because you care. And each time we choose to care for an animal we love, we can change the world, just one animal at a time. I absolutely know that you would want the very best for whatever animal you love, and it starts right there. I understand the world can sometimes feel scary. You will already know all about climate change and how important it is to protect our planet. But if we look after each other – human and animal – the future can be bright for all of us.

Above all, I want you to be inspired by the incredible stories of the superpets I've met on my journey. It is a **huge honour** to be allowed the chance to save the limb or life of an animal, and **I never take that for granted for one second. The best part of my job is seeing the love between animals and their human guardians. This love blots out all other worries, bypasses all the blockages in our hearts and burns as bright as a star.** That's why it's called 'unconditional' love – **because it has no conditions – it just 'is'.**

If we can harness this love – if we can learn the lessons of courage, of compassion, of determination and creativity that I witness daily – **we can make the planet a better place for every living creature.**

CHAPTER 1
The Beginning

I was born and raised and trained as a vet in Ireland, but I live outside London, in England, now. Though I travel within and outside the country occasionally, my time is mostly spent at my veterinary practice, which specialises in neuro-orthopaedics (muscular, skeletal and spinal issues that affect mobility and the nervous system). The animals who come to see me are usually suffering pain or disease or have been operated on already and those operations have failed and need fixing. I've met some remarkable pets and people, and I have seen both **great joy** and **sadness**.

If there's a message I'd like readers to take

from this book, aside from the fun stories about the amazing animals I've met, it's that **we share our planet with them and we should treat them as equals worthy of dignity, empathy and, above all, love.**

Wherever they live, whether they are out there in the wild in *their* homes or sitting curled up on the sofa in *your* home, we should look after every one of them. They might not speak our language, they might not have our human concerns of jobs or money or dreams of seeking acknowledgement and fame, but in the things that really matter they're the same. Animals deserve the same unconditional love that they show us.

We can learn a huge amount from animals. I know I have. They really can make us better and kinder people.

From Farm Boy to Bionic Vet

I grew up in the village of Ballyfin in County Laois in central Ireland. It's a place of cattle and sheep farming, of growing wheat, barley, grass and turnips to feed the animals. Green fields are dotted with barns and sheds, separated by hedgerows and fences. The traffic often moves slowly behind tractors on narrow roads. The horizon is ringed by the low foothills of the **Slieve Bloom Mountains**, which change colour with the conditions – pale under dappled sunshine, purple with storms and invisible in the mist. The weather can change in an instant, and you are happy for the rain on your face. It's a beautiful place, in many ways – especially in the spring, when the trees erupt with blossom, the birdsong greets the dawn and new life is everywhere in the fields, the hedges and the trees.

My daddy was a farmer, as was his before him. And though my father never said it, he likely assumed

I would end up working with animals. Coming from where I did, there was no reason to think differently. But I knew from a young age I wouldn't be a farmer and that I wanted to create and to use my **imagination** in a different way to help animals.

When I was at primary school, I couldn't read and write very well but I loved **comic books**. I was inspired by the pictures and would spend hours getting lost in their world. I also loved listening to music. I'd listen to songs on an old radio I found on a scrap heap, for which I'd made

an antenna from an old metal coat hanger. Sometimes I'd watch pop and rock stars on our wind-up television box too, where you had to put in a 50p coin to watch a programme. When I was about eleven years old, I was desperate for a guitar. But my daddy didn't really understand anything about musical instruments. He handed me a large saw for removing the horns from young cattle and told me to polish and sharpen it. I could have cried, but there was no cruelty in this gift. It was who he was and who I was expected to be. He wasn't a man of many words. He never said 'I love you' or 'I am proud of you', but I always knew he was proud of me in his own quiet way.

We lived in a stone farmhouse: my mammy and daddy, and my brother and sisters. We shared the place with mice in the skirting and birds in the roof and a stray cat who gave birth to kittens in the hay barn. Mammy wanted to get rid of the mice, so would set traps for them. Not the **humane** kind you can get today, but the sort that snap and break a rodent's neck. I used to cover them up with old clothes, hoping no poor mouse would venture nearby. My parents wouldn't have understood it, but I knew even then that the lives of the creatures around me – **big or small** – were important.

Life was not particularly easy, but my mammy and daddy always did their best. I didn't have or see much money. But I didn't feel poor, because the world I lived in was small, and no one I knew was wealthy anyway – so I didn't know any different. There was no central heating in our house, and so warmth in the winter months came from burning turf fires in the hearth and from however many layers you could stack on top of one another in bed. At night, ice would form on the inside of the windows. **I didn't like having to drag myself from my bed in the morning.**

It was my job to venture out into the fields after midnight, checking in on the sheep that were having lambs, so I have been a night owl from an early age. Then, when I knew I couldn't read and write very well, I stayed up really late studying to pass many exams. I have done so ever since, often writing books like this one you're reading now into the night. Needless to say, I'm still not a morning person! I often sleep in a bedroom at my practice and when my colleagues ring my office to say that my first patient is about to arrive, they call it **'waking the sleeping bear'** ...

Back on the farm, the work never stopped. There was *always* something to be done, whether mending a gate, trimming hooves or dipping sheep in a bath of foul-smelling fluid to prevent flies from laying eggs in their wool. If we didn't do it, the eggs would turn into maggots and eat their skin, so it was important work, but it was **extremely smelly.**

Even today I find it hard to sit still for long. I remember very few times in my youth when daddy took a day off, and we kids were expected to muck in too. **I was driving tractors in the fields at the age of nine (sometimes very badly, and I'll tell you more about that later)** and digging drainage ditches through

my teens to dry out the fields so we could grow turnips and barley for animal feed. Farming is about teamwork. The farming families of Ballyfin helped each other out, and some of my fondest memories are of that community spirit – walking cattle or sheep on country roads between one bit of the farm and another or helping with the shearing in early summer.

Our family had several patches of land, and our

main business was raising sheep and cattle. My father reared lambs and calves, before selling them on for slaughter. You might think it strange that someone who has dedicated his life to helping save the lives of animals started out watching them be raised for food, but perhaps without that experience I would have ended up somewhere quite different. I know that the **hardest time** for me was always the day the lambs were loaded into the truck and transported away. They couldn't have known their destination, but I imagined they did from their panicked bleating. *I* knew, and it left me **very sad**. These were my friends I was saying goodbye to. I still ate meat well into my adult life, though I haven't done for a long time now and there's no judgement from me on that. People should do whatever they feel is right – after all, these cattle and sheep would simply not exist if people didn't eat them. What I believe is important is how these animals are looked after when they are alive and that farming practices are as humane as they can be, meaning they treat their animals with kindness.

Caring for the cows was no less painful to me either. One of the jobs I performed as a teenage boy was de-horning cattle. It's not nice to describe, but it's one of my most powerful memories from being a boy. The young bullocks are careless with their new horns, and when they jostle, it's easy for them to injure one another, especially when they go to market. The bone saw Daddy gave me instead of a guitar was one of the tools I used. It hangs on my office wall to this day, along with a syringe and a pair of forceps, to remind me where I've come from. Forceps are metal instruments that look a bit like tweezers with handles like a scissors that help you grasp hold of small things. In this case, they were used to clasp the horn's blood vessels (the tubes that ferry blood around the body) that were spurting blood after cutting the horn off.

The process was as follows:

1. We led a young bullock into a chute.
2. The head was held steady in a gate clamp.
3. We used a syringe to inject a liquid called anaesthetic at the base of the horn to numb the nerve pain.
4. We held the bullock steady with tongs in the nose.
5. The saw was used to cut off the horn at the nub and the forceps to twist the blood vessel to stop the bleeding.

These days calves are often 'disbudded' at a younger age, before their horns have fully grown, and methods are less brutal. In fact, over the years, many farming practices have become **kinder to animals** than when I was a boy, and for that I'm glad. I strongly believe in good welfare practices for all creatures – they all deserve compassion.

You can't grow up on a farm without being faced

daily with the realities of life and death and suffering. The animals in our care might have been headed for the plate, but a good farmer tries to make their lives as comfortable as possible. Whether it was a lame calf who needs his hoof trimmed to remove a stone or a lamb with an eye infection, **we did our best to heal them**. Farmers learn to deal with many problems on their own without calling out a vet. You improvise with whatever you have at hand – stitching up wounds with a needle and thread, splinting a broken limb with some twigs and twine, administering medicines for many different conditions. Sometimes there's nothing to be done for an animal, and he or she needs to be euthanised. I watched my daddy do all of these tasks without fuss, and I grew to understand that **death was an inevitable part of life**. I wasn't afraid of it.

Daddy didn't have the luxury of loving animals in the way I did, because they were his livelihood. But he cared for them well – he *respected* them and didn't want them to suffer. I often wonder what he'd make of the *Supervet* TV programmes if he saw them or if I could give him a tour of the practice where I work now. He must have guessed when I was growing up that I'd never become a farmer, but he couldn't have imagined bionic implants in cats and dogs. He'd be impressed, I think, by the technology and how far we've come since the times of twigs and twine, but more than anything I hope he'd be proud of me for the way I treat my patients. Without him and my upbringing in Ballyfin surrounded by animals, who knows where I'd be?

Inside, I'm still the same boy who wept as the lambs were taken off in a trailer. I might mask it well, but I can't help but feel for the poorly animals who come to see me. I share their pain and that of their human companions. What I can do as a vet though, with my decades of experience, is explain the problems as clearly as possible and give them all of the options. Being a vet, like a human

doctor, is about trust. When someone enters my consulting room, they're putting a lot of faith in me and I try to repay that. I don't sugar-coat the truth, but I assure my patients, and their guardians, that I'll do everything in my power to reduce suffering and give quality of life to a poorly animal. When I can't save a life, it's horrible and I still cry.

CHAPTER 2
First Steps

'You Know What You Know'

As a young boy, I wasn't good at many things, but lambing was an exception. There's something joyful and miraculous about bringing new life into the world. Spring was lambing season, and back then lambs were born from February onwards. Those early spring days could be bleak on the farm, with snow and freezing rain. We'd take shifts – all of us in the family – to keep an eye on the pregnant ewes in the field that looked like they might have their lambs soon. **Mine was always the late shift.** It was just a case of watching to make sure there were no complications and calling Daddy if there were. Later we had a warm shed to bring the birthing ewes into, but in my younger years much of the lambing took place in the fields because we didn't have room indoors; the ewes came inside for only a couple of days after they had their lambs.

A ewe will normally have a one or two lambs, but occasionally there'll be three or, very rarely, even four. When that happens, because most ewes in the world have only two teats (which are nipples for feeding the lambs with milk), the 'spare' often has to be hand-reared for the first few days, bottle-fed to make sure it puts on enough weight to stay healthy.

If one was born too weak to stand, we'd wrap him or her in a blanket to get some warmth into the limbs. Sometimes, Daddy opened the oven door in the turf-fired range cooker and popped the lamb inside in a cardboard box for a while.

One trick a farmer knows is to place a 'spare' lamb with an ewe who's only had one. But you have to be quick to convince the mama ewe that the extra lamb is hers. You take the spare and rub it in the afterbirth that's come from the ewe. The afterbirth is the sac the ewe's lamb grows in before it is born. When the ewe smells it and licks it clean, she thinks the spare lamb is her own and a **bond is formed**.

To my daddy's amusement, I would name many of the lambs. He wouldn't have dreamt of doing such a thing. Lambs were money, simple as that. Often a farmer will spray a matching number or a letter on the side of the lamb and his or her mother, so that if they become separated in the field, the farmer can pair them up again. There was nothing like that on our farm. I thought it was **mayhem**, with lambs and ewes all mixed together, especially if we were moving them from one field to another. But my daddy could always tell instinctively who matched with whom. When I asked him once how he did it, he turned to me with a little sideways smile and said simply, 'You know what you know.'

I suppose it was just an intuition, from years of experience with sheep. They didn't need names, but he could tell them apart. And I've often thought of that phrase since. So much of working with animals relies on experience. No two animals — much like no two humans — are the same, and every operation I perform is a little bit different. When I cut a patient open, there are very often surprises. I have learned from each and every one.

When I was working as a large-animal vet in my younger days, just after I graduated from vet school in 1990, it couldn't have been further from my job now. My trusty bits of equipment were simply a stethoscope

(for listening to a heartbeat), a thermometer
(for measuring temperature) and my own senses.
I travelled between farms on little sleep, often
popping into a farmhouse which had a telephone,
responding to yet another emergency beep on my
pager (there were no mobile phones back then),
to tend to pigs and cows, goats and sheep, and
even the odd horse. I had to try to form a quick
connection with the animal – using my eyes to
inspect, my fingers to probe, my ears to
hear their complaints or a rattle in their chest,
and even my nose to smell an animal's breath
for signs of disease.

In my work today, I often need to put an animal on
a drip, which is a short plastic tube with a needle
on one end and a bag on the other. It is inserted
into the vein, so that fluids and medicines can
travel directly into the bloodstream. This helps
with dehydration and recovery from any one of many

diseases like gut or lung infections. The equipment we use now is always sterile, which means it's bacteria free. Bacteria are micro-organisms that cause infection, so it's really important that they don't get into the bloodstream. But back on the farm, we didn't have readily available equipment.

Instead, I would carefully measure out some table salt and some baking soda into a saucepan of boiling water. I cut the bottom off a large plastic bottle to act as a funnel and attached it to an orange tube called a flutter valve, which ran to a needle in the jugular vein in the animal's neck. The farmers often asked me how I knew how much salt or baking soda to put in the drip. Well, I had some great teachers in old-school veterinary medicine, for which I shall be forever grateful. They taught me about 'instinct' in being a vet and how 'you know what you know'. I've carried this sense of intuition through to present day.

Recently, a Weimaraner puppy came to me – a sleek, silver-furred, blue-eyed handsome chap called Tito. Poor Tito's rear end had been run over by a van. Both hind legs were broken, but the worst injury was where the head of one of his **femurs** (thigh bones) had fractured off within the hip joint itself, which is called an intra-articular fracture. If I couldn't fix this particular fracture, it wouldn't matter if the other fractures in his hind legs were mended – he wouldn't be able to move them without pain.

The challenge with such a fracture is that you have to hold the neck of the femur bone on the

fractured head like holding the dome of a mushroom against the inside of an eggshell. The eggshell is the fractured off cap of the head and the flared neck of the femur is the mushroom. The surgical 'trick' is to drive four pins from the dome of the mushroom, back out through the mushroom stem, then you flip the mushroom back into the eggshell, and drill the pins back the opposite way in the shape of a wigwam. They have to be drilled into the softer parts of the bone, but can't stick out the other side, which would be through the **cartilage** surface into the joint. Where our limb bones move relative to each other – **that's called a joint** – the ends of the bones are coated in shiny tissue called cartilage and lubricated by fluid, so that movement is smooth. You can't *see* where the pin ends, but rather you just have to *feel* the moment the pin goes through the bony edge of the head cap, and not through the softer cartilage.

There is another way, using 3D scanning to see

the pins as they are driven in. But over the years, I've never found the need to do so. To take X-ray images that make up the 3D scans, you have to wear a gown made of lead to protect from the radiation, which

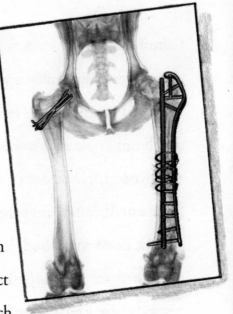

hurts my back. I am also forever blessed that I can 'feel' and 'sense' where an implant is inside a bone – much like a guitarist knows where the strings are without looking. Luckily, a CT scan after Tito's operation showed that all four pins of the 'wigwam' had skewered the femoral head cap exactly the right amount, and had not punctured the joint surface.

Afterwards, as Tito recovered in the ward, my intern colleague asked me how I'd been able to judge it so precisely. I simply nodded knowingly and said, 'You know what you know.'

The Lamb

It was on a very cold morning in February, when I was ten years old, that I headed out into the darkness of the night to check the ewes in the field. I did a headcount and realised I was one short. When this happened, the most likely scenario was that a sheep had hidden away somewhere to have her lambs. I walked around each side of the field, looking in every nook and cranny of the hedgerows by the moonlight. I finally found her. She had rolled down into one of the drainage ditches that surrounded the field. The poor girl was near-drowned already, her lower half in the muddy water, her head **gasping for breath** over the surface. It was clear to see that she was trapped and exhausted.

I knew I wouldn't have the strength to get her out – a pregnant sheep weighs enough as is, let alone bogged down and soaked through. Far too heavy for a skinny lad like me to haul up. But I thought there was a chance I might save the lamb inside her, so I jumped down into the freezing water too. Feeling beneath the surface with hands almost numb already, I felt her little one trapped in the area of the body lambs come out of, the **birth canal**. The lamb's head was lodged under her **pelvis** (the rectangular bone structure that connects the spine to the hind legs). It took some fiddling, but I managed to pull the lamb out and I fell back into the ditch, **cradling her in my arms**. Though warm, she wasn't moving at all.

This was not uncommon. Mucus gets lodged in the lamb's airways and needs to be dislodged. I crawled up the bank and went through the motions I'd seen my father do dozens of times. Gripping the lamb by the rear legs with one hand, I swung her back and forth, slapping her chest each time with my other. It looks rough, but the idea is to loosen any blockages and get the heart pumping. On this occasion, it didn't work.

Next, I held her and used some reeds to try to

clear her nostrils. Still nothing. Finally, I bent my mouth to her nose and tried to **suck the mucus out**. Gross, I know, but farming, like vet work, often is. I tried and tried, applying all the tricks of the trade. In the end, I had to accept that the poor lamb was dead. In the back of my mind, I was worried I'd be in trouble for my failure, but I often blamed myself for such things. Really there was no fault involved.

The ewe was still panting hard though, and that meant there was quite possibly another lamb inside her. So, it was back into the freezing ditch water. And **I was right** – this one had his bum facing me instead of his head, but I finally managed to pull him out too. He was lifeless as well. I tried to save him too. And – thank goodness – he gave a spluttering breath. I was too tired to be overjoyed, and there was still the problem of the trapped ewe. I left the newborn gasping for air on the frozen grass for a moment and I entered the water again, determined to get the mother out. It must have been her desperation to be near her lamb more than my spindly armed strength, but she finally clambered up on to the bank. I picked up the lamb, trying to keep him warm against the biting cold of the freezing night breeze, and made for the shed, the ewe trailing after me. I was soaked to the skin, but triumphant. At least I'd saved one.

I plodded back up the field, my Wellingtons crunching the frozen grass underfoot. **Then disaster struck.** In my hurry, and with the darkness, I slipped on the frosty grass, losing hold of the weak little lamb. As I sprawled on the earth, so did he, hitting the ground hard. And right there, lying in the mud, I saw him take his last breath. The ewe, a moment ago trotting wearily alongside us, tried to lick some life back into his limp body, but it was in vain. He too was dead. My only job was to keep the new lambs safe and well and I had utterly failed. I lay on the ground, looked up at the star-filled sky and cried my heart out.

I've always loved comic books about heroes on a quest for justice, often with superpowers. My favourites were Spiderman, Batman, Wolverine, Captain Marvel and Captain America. If my life were a comic strip, and 'Supervet' was the hero, this would be his origin story. But on that freezing night, all I could do was weep. I was no hero. I was a failure. Worthless, I thought. Pathetic. And here were two dead lambs and a grieving confused ewe to prove it. I lay on my back in the frozen grass, looking up at all the stars in heaven, picking the brightest one and wishing that I could be more strong, more brave and more clever.

Soon after, I invented my very own superhero who would be all of those things and who would save all the broken animals. His name was Vetman.[1] He would go on to have many adventures, all made up in my head. Thinking

---

[1] Vetman didn't just stay in my head! You can read his adventures in a book I wrote called *Vetman and his Bionic Animal Clan*.

of him gave me strength to keep going when things were tough.

Later in my real life, among the many miracle treatments and joyous recoveries, and the animal companions returning to their families, there have been animals I couldn't help or make better. And it's a lesson I'm still learning – that sometimes animals die and that endings can't always be happy.

Failure is what makes us human. It makes us strive to do better. Take your failures and use them as fuel to fire you toward whatever dream you have. If you have never failed, you have never tried hard enough, and if you have ever succeeded through anything other than repeated failure, it generally doesn't last, because you haven't learned enough humility to make it last.

Pirate and Trust

When families bring their companions to see me at my practice, I am always **honest** about what I can and can't achieve, and what I feel is in the best interests of the animal patient. Though I'm paid by the human, the animal is my main concern – that's part of the oath we vets have to take – the animal's welfare comes first and one must never 'do harm'. All treatments have to be 'ethically balanced' – what *can* be done is not always what *should* be done. If an operation is likely not in the best interests of the patient and could cause more problems or pain without hope of recovery in a reasonable time frame, I won't attempt it. It's not fair to put any animal through unnecessary suffering.

Many young people come along with their parents, and I see first-hand what their animal companions mean to them – they are their family members. Often, the kids I see have grown up with their dogs and cats, so they're as close as a brother or a sister. I'm open with them too. I'm not a miracle worker.

I also know personally how strong these relationships can be. As well as the cows and sheep on the farm, we had a sheepdog too – a black and white collie called Dingy. But it was another dog, a puppy my father brought home when I was a very young child with whom I really bonded. We called him Pirate, because he had a white face with a black patch around one eye. Like many sheepdogs, Pirate was a bundle of energy with a zest for life. Collies have a natural instinct to herd, but they still have to be trained, and my father took Pirate out in the fields with Dingy from a young age. He took to herding like a duck to water.

Daddy treated Pirate like any other animal, so there was no coming in our farmhouse. When he wasn't working, he was kept on a long chain in a nearby cattle shed. We'd never dream of keeping a dog like that now, but the thinking back then was that a dog on a leash when he was resting had more energy to burn when loose in the fields. For me, Pirate was special.

I would sneak into the cattle shed where he slept at night and cuddle him. I'd share my secrets, hopes and fears. I'd read him my favourite comic books and tell him the stories I'd made up in my head about Vetman, who flew around the world helping animals of every kind. Soon Pirate was part of the stories too, Vetman's companion on

their heroic quests, along with a lion with a very big heart. Pirate would listen patiently – animals tend to be much better at listening than people, in my experience. With few other children to play with in our rural community, Pirate became my best friend in the whole world. We built our own imaginary world together.

I was so very lucky to have Pirate in my life. Some bad things happened when I was a young child which meant that I didn't trust humans very much. But I could always trust Pirate. He was always there for me, I hugged him and he licked away my tears and tried always to ease my pain.

Later, when I was twelve, I began to attend the local secondary school, Patrician College in Ballyfin. This grand building was a boarding school which also accepted day pupils like me, who would come each morning and leave in the afternoon. The first day I rode my bicycle up to the pillared entrance, I felt hopelessly out of place. My previous school had been three rooms, one for each age group, so Patrician College looked huge and daunting.

It was worse inside. I rapidly I discovered that my standard of learning up until that point had been poor. I couldn't read or write well and my maths was terrible. Along with my humble upbringing on the farm, this meant **I became a target for the bullies**. Many of them came from cities and big towns in Ireland and they called me a *culchie*, which means 'a person from rural areas' or 'uncultured'.

I don't think that was all that led to me being singled out. I was out of my depth. Shy and sensitive, I struggled to speak my thoughts. I'm sure the boys who picked on me had their own problems to make them behave how they did, but at the time I only feared them. That first day, I cycled home and went straight to Pirate and hugged him tight. I was confused more than angry and didn't tell my mammy or daddy. Not because they wouldn't understand, but because *I* didn't. I suppose I thought that what was happening was somehow my fault, like when bad things happened to me before. Just as with the lambs I failed to save, I wasn't clever enough or strong enough to matter.

At night, Pirate listened, like he always did. He stared into my eyes with his bottomless dark gaze and, as always, **he licked away my tears**.

The bullying started with name-calling, but it grew worse. Pushes and shoves became wedgies (when someone sneaks up on you and hoists your underpants up hard, which might sound funny, but,

I assure you, is not if you're on the receiving end). I never fought back. Instead, I tried to stay out of their way and dedicated myself to schoolwork. There was so much catching up to do. So much I didn't know. But with **the help of some inspirational teachers**, I began to understand subjects better, especially those that involved the real world, like chemistry, physics and biology. I struggled with maths, and still do unless the numbers have concrete meaning in the world – the length and weight of an implant for a certain sized dog or the dosage of a medication.

Before I attended secondary school, I had no idea that I couldn't read properly. My primary school had been good at teaching the stories and lessons of the Bible, but not much else. I learned to read properly for the first time at college, and this opened up a world I never knew existed. I loved poetry and plays especially – Dylan Thomas and Oscar Wilde were my favourites. Now I devoured books and hid them all over the place

– in the hayshed and in the orchard in a plastic bag. I suppose I hoped that if I could fit in better, the bullying might stop. Unfortunately, I was wrong. Now I was a target because I was always the boy with my hand up to answer a question or poring over my books all the time – day and night. The hard worker. The 'teacher's pet'. The 'swot', as they called me.

Behind the school was an old quarry and at lunchtime a group of boys often threw me in it, with a few punches for good measure. Sewage from the nearby farm flowed into the quarry, so you can imagine how **horrible** it was. Again, I never tried to fight them because I just wanted them to lose interest and end the ordeal. I got used to dealing with cuts and bruises from being beaten up.

There were less physically painful incidents which hurt me more. One time a group of bullies pounced on me while I rode home and **stole my bike**. By jamming the wheels into a cattle grid and bending the frame back and forth, they wrecked it completely. On another occasion they spilled milk all over my precious textbooks and notepads, ruining the stories, diagrams and drawings I'd worked on for hours. One person even climbed into the ceiling space above my desk to **drip ink on me as I worked**. Back then I was scared of speaking to anyone or making a scene. It was easier just to disappear. To this day, I can't stand bullying, and I'd tell anyone suffering it, **'You're not alone. Talk to a grown-up** and make sure that they understand how much it is affecting you.' I promise you it will turn out OK in the end if you learn to use your experience and your fear like fuel to propel you forward and achieve great things. I believe that bullies are just people who can't look in the mirror.

My only solaces through these hard times were Pirate and my schoolwork. By now I'd decided that my future lay away from farming and in veterinary medicine. But to get to vet college, I'd need good grades at school. So I threw myself into the work harder than ever before. I especially fell in love with biology and the complex workings of the body.

Luckily, I found a secret place to hide during lunchtimes, when otherwise the bullies might have tracked me down. There was an old **gardener's cottage** on the school grounds.

Abandoned, full of cobwebs, with a leaking thatched roof. There I made friends with a visiting robin and a nest of swallows, and I read my schoolbooks in peace, disappearing into my own world. It became the same at home.

I'd rush back after school, do my chores and spend some time with Pirate, before wishing him 'nighty-night' and getting back to the books.

I didn't make any close friendships at Patrician College over the five years I attended, but it didn't matter to me. I had Pirate, and I had my books.

The work paid off, because each year I won some academic prizes, which acted as a marker of progress in my head, and at the end of my time there I passed my exams and was offered places at university to study either veterinary or human medicine. It wasn't a difficult decision – the animals were calling me. My life was about to change forever as I spread my wings and left Ballyfin.

In the first year of my university training in Dublin, where I was buried once more in learning, Pirate passed away. He was a grand old age of fifteen years, which is good for any dog. My father didn't tell me until much later. I think that, despite his tough farmer ways, he knew what Pirate had meant to me throughout those lonely years and he didn't want to disrupt my studies. I know he too was much fonder of Pirate than he ever let on. Pirate was more than just a herder of sheep, that's for sure.

Nighty-night, my loyal and trusted friend.

DECIDING WHAT IS RIGHT

When it comes to bionic implants or 'superpets', it's very important to emphasise something called **ethics**, which means to do the right thing. This involves always **doing the best for the animals** I care for. That means that though it might be *possible* to do something, it doesn't mean it's the right thing or that we *should* do it. For example, though I can perform an operation called 'limb salvage', using bionic implants to replace part of a leg, many dogs and cats will be able to have a really great quality of life on three legs. So, if I am confident their life won't be negatively impacted by only having three limbs, the right thing to do may be to amputate (meaning to remove that leg). There are many factors to consider, which include deciding what's morally best for the animal and what is practically and financially best for the family.

Sometimes it's a matter of opinion too. Vets disagree with me all the time, and some think my operations are too extreme. They call it 'over-treatment'. We all have different opinions on what the 'kindest' option might be. For example, some vets think putting an animal to sleep can be the best 'treatment' for many conditions, because it stops the pain, instead of undertaking any risks of surgery. But with my experience of surgical procedures in hundreds of animals over many years, I often disagree.

That's not to say I offer surgery all the time.

When you watch my television show, it might look like this is all I do, but that's just because those tends to be the more interesting bits the TV crew want to film. Sometimes I might recommend medicine or limb amputation or sadly putting the patient to sleep when there's nothing else that can be done. I do the right thing according to the morals inside my own heart and mind.

Throughout life, there will always be people who agree with you and those who don't, and that's OK. People can only see things from their perspective and their experience. They haven't performed the surgeries or spoken with the families of these animals as I have. I always tell myself that the only real truth is the truth inside of yourself and that you need to be at peace in your soul that you are doing the right thing.

As we will explore later in chapter 10, sadly many of the operations I perform on sick animals have already been performed on healthy animals during animal testing. This is when companies test medicines and treatments on animals, before using them on humans (it's called an animal experiment). Animals don't even benefit from this testing, so even though dogs and cats are in pain and need such treatments, they often can't get them. And even if they eventually can have these drugs and implants, it's many years after they have been made available for humans, since the companies need to make their research investment back from human patients first. There are thousands of drugs and implants that animals have been sacrificed for, to give to humans, that are just not available for my animal patients who really need them. Many vets feel that an experiment on an animal for human benefit is acceptable but giving that same drug or implant in a well-controlled study to an animal that really needs it is not acceptable. In my work I always try to see it from the point of view of the animal and to be their advocate. They can't speak our language but they do talk to us . . . through love.

If you decide to become a vet, the animals and families are in your hands. The job involves making many tough decisions and you have to decide what you think is the best and the right thing to do. But there's one massive pay-off – and that is that when you can make an animal better, when you see wagging tails and smiling families, it's the greatest happiness in the world.

CHAPTER 3
Meet the Team!

Many children I meet want to become a vet and ask me for advice. The first thing I'd always say is that **if it's your passion, you should follow it.** That applies to everything you do in life, but always be aware that you should never follow your passion just to make money! Try to follow your passion whilst making a difference in the world, and in that way, you can achieve your wildest dreams in the best way possible. The second thing I'd say is that it takes a lot of time, determination and hard work to become a vet. Not only do you need good grades at school, but there's five or six years of basic training afterwards, just like being a human doctor.

Even then, there's additional training to become a specialist in a particular area. The field is changing all the time, with scientific advancement and new ways of doing things. Not to mention all the knowledge that experience brings – the patients in my care teach me things every day and I'll never stop learning. **Every day is a school day**.

I've worked in many different jobs as a vet. From large-animal farm work, to equine (horse) care, to being a primary care companion animal vet, to being a surgical specialist in neuro-orthopaedics today.

When I first qualified as a vet, most practices were 'general practices', which meant that they dealt with all kinds of animals from hamsters to horses. These practices are now very rare, and most vets and nurses

decide that they want to work with a particular group of animals, for example either:

- ❧ Horses.

- ❧ Farm animals.

- ❧ Companion animals like cats and dogs, which may also include 'small furries' such as rabbits, guinea pigs and hamsters.

- ❧ Exotics, which include snakes, lizards, tortoises and parrots, and can include small furry animals too.

There are also other career pathways after vet school, like caring for wild animals, working in labs for the pharmaceutical and implant industries, or perhaps in areas that cover both animals and people such as One Health. The One Health approach looks at the health and wellbeing of all living beings. By researching animals and ecosystems, we can learn about things like how diseases transfer between animals and humans and make advances to medical science. However, these advances are often designed to benefit human health. But my life's work is an approach I have adopted called One Medicine, where animals and humans have equal significance and there is a fair two-way exchange of ideas that helps both animals and humans. The pledge of One Medicine is to reduce the number of animals used in experiments by studying naturally occurring diseases like cancer or arthritis in both animals and humans, so that everyone benefits. It also aims to allow the drugs and medical technology we use for humans to be available for the animals we love too. You will find more about One Medicine on page 256.

When vets see any animal as a first port of call, their practices are called 'primary care practices'. These vets are the first in line when animals are unwell and either the animal is brought to them or they visit the animal wherever they live.

Primary care practice is where you may take your cat or dog to get vaccinations or flea treatments, to have a microchip inserted, for stomach bugs, ear infections, teeth cleaning or straightforward operations like **neutering**. Most also provide X-ray imaging and many primary care practices try to provide more advanced services too.

When training to work in primary care, it's a really good idea for vets to get lots of experience with the type of animal they want to work with. You see so many patients with every ailment under the sun, so if a primary care vet is going to take on advanced surgery, it's very important they have lots of training and experience. Sadly, I have seen many problems with patients who have had surgery by a vet who didn't have the proper training, or didn't use proper technique, and this means the poor animal needed another surgery to fix what went wrong. Any surgery can go wrong for any surgeon, including me – but you must always have the proper training, be honest with the family about your skill level and work in the best interest of the animal.

When advanced treatment is needed for an animal beyond what a primary care practice can offer, then 'specialist' care is often looked for. This means that the primary care vet should recommend or 'refer' the patient to a 'specialist' or 'referral' hospital. This is often in a different practice, but sometimes specialists will visit the primary care vets too, travelling from practice to practice with all their kit.

Veterinary practice as a vocation has changed a lot since I started as a vet in the early 1990s. When I began, I worked until I had to sleep. I often got woken up in the night by calls to a birthing cow or sheep in difficulty – and then I started all over again early the next morning. That kind of lifestyle doesn't really exist any more for the vast majority

of vets. Today there are emergency primary care centres which will see sick animals in the evenings, at night-time and at weekends. And there are rotas, or schedules, to allow time off if vets work over weekends. **A balance between work and life is now considered very important for a vet's mental health.**

I haven't been good at this balance myself. I've always been a night owl, and I often stay up late finishing reports and paperwork, or designing and planning implants for future cases. By the time I'm finished, there's often no point heading home, so I sleep at the surgery during the week, in a small bedroom next to my office, with my cat friends Ricochet and Excalibur for company. That's always been OK for me, but I wouldn't encourage anyone to follow my example!

DIFFERENT KINDS OF

General Practice

Veterinary practices that deal with all kinds of animals.

Primary Care Practice

The first port of call for sick animals. There are primary care practices in most towns and many villages, so you're never far away from one. They sometimes provide their own emergency service for out of hours too.

Out-of-Hours/Emergency Practice

A practice set up specially to see cases after normal working hours, which is in the evenings, at night-time or at weekends. This kind of practice might rent space from a local primary care practice during its out of hours or can be in an entirely different

VETERINARY PRACTICES

building in your village, town or city. It will have special agreements with many primary care practices nearby to look after their patients when they are closed.

Small or Companion Animal Practice

In small animal practice you can become part of a community and get to know families as they get to know their animal friends. You see bouncy puppies and playful kittens getting their first jabs, and deaf old dogs who can barely shuffle through the door of the practice. Small furry animals can also often be seen.

Equine Practice

Some vets decide to look after just horses and ponies in 'equine' practice.

Large or Farm Animal Practice

A practice that looks after pigs, sheep, goats, cattle and other hoofed animals like llamas.

Exotic Animal Practice

These vets look after animals such as snakes, lizards, tortoises, various kinds of birds and sometimes zoo animals or those from wildlife parks. Like some small animal practices, exotic animal practices can also see small furries like rabbits, hamsters and guinea pigs. Wild animals can be seen by both small and exotic animal practices, and some sanctuaries have their own vets.

Specialist Care/Referral Hospital

If there's an issue a vet feels they can't deal with, they can send, or *refer*, the patient to a specialist, like my practice, Fitzpatrick Referrals. So, a family can't just ring up a practice like mine or come to see me or my colleagues directly – they must first see a primary care practice vet to be referred. People often think because I am a vet (and because I am on television!) that I know everything about every part of every animal. Nothing could be further from the truth. I'm a specialist, and so know a lot about only some parts of the body and not about other parts. It's been a very long time since I operated on an ear canal or on the belly of a dog, for example. Earwax and guts are not for me – different horses for different courses!

My Practice

The practice I run is called **Fitzpatrick Referrals**. The name means that patients are sent on ('referred') to me and my team once a primary care vet or the pet's family have decided they need the specialist treatment we can provide. Either the vet sends them to the specialist or the family request to be sent.

Fitzpatrick Referrals began as a derelict farm – four old tumbledown buildings in the countryside. Now

it's a **state-of-the-art practice** specialising in neuro-orthopaedics. It's a place for animals to come when they've got skeletal or muscular problems that are affecting how they move. Sometimes this is caused by the wear and tear of age, or illness like cancer and **inflammation**, or **degenerative** problems (problems that get worse over time), but often the animals that come to see me have been involved in accidents, such as being hit by a car.

There are about 170 people working at Fitzpatrick Referrals. There are often more than 90 of the team in the practice on any given day, and I couldn't do my job without their brilliant support. We work in shifts and there's always a team of people on duty, even overnight. Just as the parts of a body have to work in harmony, so does my practice team. Everyone has an important role in making a dog or

cat's visit as happy and safe as possible.

As the head of surgery, it's my responsibility to ensure the best care for the animals who come through the door. But there are plenty of other roles at the practice and they are all equally important – a chain is only as strong as its weakest link.

Very Important Roles in a Specialist Practice Other than Vets

Ward Clinical Care Assistants

These assistants feed and care for the patients. They clean the kennels, pick up the poo and clean up the wee and vomit! They monitor patients after operations, cuddle them, talk to them and give them their medication.

Theatre Clinical Care Assistants

These are the team members who prepare the patients and the theatre (operation room), so that everything is as efficient and safe as possible. They clip the hair or fur and sterilise the skin of the patient, they sterilise the equipment and deliver it to the surgical team and they make sure that our kit and tools, such as heating blankets, towels, suction and drapes are all where they should be. When I operate, I think of the set-up like a racing car coming into a pit stop – everything and everyone needs to be ready to go. I expect my team to be ready when I ask for tools, such as drills, saws or screwdrivers. That's why we can perform a total hip replacement, beginning to end, in less than one hour. It's all about the teamwork!

Theatre and Ward Nurses

Theatre nurses are trained veterinary nurses who prepare cases for operations and sometimes help the vet with the operations too, while ward nurses look after the medical and recuperation needs of animals in the recovery wards. Nurses are critical to the patient journey and perform many jobs that often vets get the credit for. They work very hard to make sure that every single aspect of the patient journey is safe, efficient and compassionate, for which they deserve huge credit.

Like vets, veterinary nurses can go on to achieve further specialist training, such as in anaesthesia (making sure animals are asleep and don't feel pain when they are operated on), critical care (emergencies) or even in management roles (making sure groups of nurses and care assistants are all doing their jobs and are happy).

Radiographers

Radiographers operate the advanced diagnostic imaging (ADI) department where the CT and MRI scans are obtained. More on this on page 93. Without these images, none of what I do would be possible.

Rehabilitation Practitioners

These are the people who assist the recovery of patients after bone, joint or spinal surgery. They also treat conditions like osteoarthritis ('osteo' means bone, 'arth' means joint, and 'itis' refers to inflammation; so osteoarthritis means inflamed joints).

Hydrotherapists help dogs and cats to swim in a hydrotherapy pool and also aid dogs on the underwater treadmill, where a belt moves underfoot while the water in the tank provides resistance for strength and muscle building. Hydrotherapy means 'to treat with water', and the idea is that the water helps animals to float, which takes pressure off vulnerable joints and limbs. We have life jackets to fit different sized animals, from the skinniest cat to the beefiest dog, and use a harness to stop them from paddling off or getting distressed. Unfortunately, it can't stop them from going for a poo in the pool!

Physiotherapists create plans for various kinds of exercises, where either the animal moves the limb themselves, or the physiotherapist moves the limb or joint for them to improve the range of motion. They also use medical laser, electrical muscle stimulation and shockwave therapy to reduce pain and improve mobility.

Regenerative Medicine Practitioners

Regenerative Medicine Practitioners are trained to

grow stem cells in a laboratory from **bone marrow** (a soft spongy tissue found in the center of most bones) or from pericytes (the small cells that surround blood vessels) and other cells that live in fat tissue which can be easily harvested from most animals. Stem cells are cells that can renew and can also be grown in certain laboratory conditions into other types of cells in the body. This is called 'multi-potency' because such cells can serve many functions. They can reduce swelling and pain due to inflammation inside joints by pumping out molecules called **anti-inflammatory** cytokines into the fluid that lubricates joints, or they can be grown into other useful cells such as cartilage or bone cells to heal injuries.

Biomechanical Engineers

These are the people who help me to design the implants that can transform the lives of injured and diseased patients. Without these engineers, there would be no bionic implants and no innovative solutions to very challenging problems. They make calculations, create drawings and work with machinists who manufacture the implants to the highest specification.

Support Colleagues

The support team vary from people who are involved in making sure infections in the practice are minimised, to the people in triage who log the cases referred to us and match them with a vet, to those in reception who book appointments and speak to primary care vets and clients on the phone – as well as to people who take care of management, money and maintenance of our facilities. Without any of these dedicated folks, Fitzpatrick Referrals would grind to a halt.

Interns and Residents

Interns are veterinary surgeons who have graduated from vet schools across the world and who would like to pursue a career as a specialist surgeon. They spend one year working and training with us.

Residents are veterinary surgeons who have some experience working in a practice after veterinary school and have often already completed a couple of one-year internships. Then they apply for residency positions which are intensive three-year courses that prepare them to take very difficult examinations to become specialists. My practice trains specialist surgeons, but there are other specialities such as cancer, skin conditions, eye issues, dentistry or exotic companion animal care, for example.

So, the term 'veterinary surgeon' is a bit misleading since all vets are legally allowed to perform surgery, but their level of training or skill varies dramatically, even if they have certificates of further training. Ultimately, specialist surgeons have had the most thorough training and experience and are taught how to deal with the most difficult challenges in specific surgeries.

Two Furry Heroes

We're a family at the practice, and the team pull together for the good of our patients, who often need care 24/7. Sometimes, even the animal companions of our work colleagues help out too! When William the cat came to us, having been hit by a car, he'd already lost a lot of blood and needed an urgent transfusion (blood passed from one animal to another) before we could operate on his broken bones. Cat blood comes in three types, so we did a blood test to see what type William was. It was Type A, the most common. One of our nurses volunteered her own cat, Orson, as a donor, so we drew blood from his vein and injected it into William. Orson got lots of treats and a warm bed to recover, and William pulled through his ordeal as well. We're all one big family — human and animal; we pull together and look after each other.

CHAPTER 4
Welcome to Our Specialist Practice!

When an animal is referred to Fitzpatrick Referrals by a primary care vet, it's usually because something is going badly wrong in their bones, joints or spine, because we specialise in orthopaedics and neurosurgery. Such illnesses can be age-related, or because of an accident. When I learned the anatomy of cats and dogs at veterinary college, we used model skeletons as well as dissection of the bodies of dogs and cats that were donated after death. I still have real donated cat and dog skeletons in my consulting room! It means I can show families where the various bones are and where the problems their pet is having might be.

Looking Inside

In the past, it was hard to see exactly what was going on inside a poorly animal – beneath the fur and skin, the internal workings were a mystery. These days, we have a range of equipment to look inside. When faced with a new patient, I might have a good idea what the problem is from examining him or her with my eyes or feeling with my fingers, but to be sure, I'll look inside using 'diagnostic imaging'.

There are lots of ways to look inside an animal as illustrated in this box below, and images are interpreted by experienced vets, surgical specialist vets or specialist vet radiologists.

DIAGNOSTIC IMAGING

1. X-ray images (or 'radiographs', often just called 'X-rays') are very common. You may have had one yourself in hospital if you've ever broken a bone. X-rays are beams of high-energy radiation that pass through many kinds of solid material. X-ray images are shadow-pictures of what the high energy beam passes through, recorded on old-fashioned film or nowadays on digital 'plates'. They were discovered in the nineteenth century by accident, and doctors quickly realised how they could be used to find broken bones and bullets inside injured soldiers. X-ray images are usually obtained by vets and nurses, and our patients are sedated or anaesthetised so they remain still.

2. A CT (computed tomography) scan is an image of an area of a body made up of many X-ray images on a computer, like a 3D puzzle. The animal is

sedated or anaesthetised and so remains still, and is then placed on a bed which moves into the 'hole' of a doughnut-shaped CT scanner. X-ray beam generators spin around the doughnut, taking hundreds of X-ray images of the animal's insides, like layers or slices. A computer then uses these images to create 3D models of all the animal's tissues, including bone, internal organs and blood vessels. CT scans are usually acquired by radiographers who are experts with these complex machines. Special dye can also be used to highlight certain structures, like clumps of tumour cells, which can be treated with high doses of radiation from another machine called a 'linear accelerator'.

3. Fluoroscopy is a kind of X-ray imaging which is often carried out by surgeons in real time while they operate. This can help when placing metal implants, for example, or when they are using

long instruments inside the patient to deliver stents (special expanding scaffolding tubes) to unblock arteries, or cancer drugs, for example, that need to be applied to a particular area which can't be seen from the outside.

4. An MRI (magnetic resonance imaging) scan is an image made using radio waves and powerful magnetic fields to show the body's insides in 3D and in real time. The machine makes a 'proton map' of each slice of an organ and when all the slices of the patient are joined together, like slices in a loaf of bread, we have a full picture of various body parts. MRI scans are also usually acquired by radiographers.

5. Ultrasound scanners can be operated by vets, nurses and radiographers. They create an image of the inside of the body by using high-frequency

sound waves, which travel through tissue and
fluid, and bounce back differently from dense or
less dense surfaces to create an image.

6. Surgeons can also use tiny, rigid fibre-optic
   scopes inside joints (arthroscopy) or inside the
   belly (laparoscopy) or the chest (thoracoscopy),
   which are attached to cameras. These cameras
   project images on to big screens so that a vet
   can operate keyhole surgery with tiny incisions.
   Flexible fibre-optic scopes with cameras attached
   can be used for looking in places like the nose,
   throat and food pipe, or even up the other end
   of the digestive system too!

I couldn't do my job without diagnostic imaging, but as I say to the people who train with me, there is no imaging in the world that can replace clinical skill and a thorough examination.

Working out what's wrong with a patient is called 'making a diagnosis' and for this a thorough external examination is needed, including feeling with your hands and using tools like a thermometer to take temperature or a stethoscope to listen to the heart. 'Gait assessments' are very important in my role as a neuro-orthopaedic surgeon, which can be as simple as observing the cat or dog walking. We also have a computerised walkway which tells us exactly how much pressure is placed on the individual pads of each foot. As you might imagine, cats especially aren't the most co-operative patients, so sometimes it's also helpful to see videos of dogs and cats at home. This is also particularly important in working or athlete dogs who need to perform to a high level. They may have a problem which is only obvious when they're doing certain things like jumping or running.

I'll also talk to the animal's human companion to find out what is called a 'clinical history.' Maybe the dog or cat has had an accident or their behaviour might have changed. Are they walking differently, making strange noises or not eating or going to the toilet as normal? Unlike humans, animals can't talk and tell you where 'it hurts', but that doesn't mean they can't communicate with their body language. For example, if they can't feel me pinching a paw, that means the nerves are likely damaged. If they try to nip me when I touch a spot, that means it's likely sore. Some very well-behaved dogs will just simply quiver or lick their lips if you touch a painful spot. **A good vet can interpret the body language of their patients.**

Sometimes I'm like an electrician visiting a house where the lights won't turn on. Something has gone wrong, but it's not always clear at first. I need to talk to the homeowners, ask what they've done or seen and then I need to inspect the switches and run some tests. I might even have to start drilling holes or knocking down parts of walls to check the wiring! Other tests are also important, such as taking a blood sample. There are hundreds of tests which can be performed on blood samples, depending on what a vet is looking for. Analysis of urine or faeces samples (posh words for wee and poo!) can also be very important.

Diagnostic imaging and blood tests can also be useful to explain to the human companion what's happening to their animal friend. I know the anatomy of a dog or cat like the back of my hand, but most of my patients' guardians do not. Scans also let us work out a way to fix problems or prepare for what we'll find when we cut open the patient in theatre. Some operations may be quite simple, such as draining fluid from a swelling or stitching up a wound. Or bones might need to be fixed after a breakage using pins or plates and screws. However, sometimes surgery is far more complicated. An implant may be designed to take the place of a bone or to hold apart two bones that are rubbing together. Using a CT scan we can make the implant ahead of time to exactly the right size and shape, then slot it into place once the operation begins. This is known as a **customised implant**. Then, after an operation, another CT scan can be performed to see if the implants are in the correct position and that the repair has gone as planned.

You Won't Feel a Thing

There are lots of specialist jobs at Fitzpatrick Referrals and among the most important are the team in anaesthesia. An anaesthetist is a specialist trained vet who gives chemicals to an animal by injection or as a gas through the mouth to help them relax or causes them to fall deeply asleep. They also have many other ways to manage pain. Often nurses will give anaesthetic too, with the help of a vet, and generally theatre nurses monitor the anaesthetic throughout the operation. Anaesthetic stops voluntary nerve signals travelling from the brain to the body or the body to the brain. It can be a 'local' injection which means it targets a certain area only locally and so the patient stays awake. Or a 'general' anaesthetic where the animal is made completely unconscious. There isn't any operation that I perform on dogs or cats that does not require either deep sedation for minor procedures or general anaesthesia for any form of surgery. It doesn't matter whether it's a short or a long procedure – the most important thing is that my patient **does not feel pain**. We measure this carefully. We want the animal to be asleep for just the right amount of time, and we make absolutely sure medicine is given afterwards for pain control too.

Cutting

In any given work day I might be:

- Seeing acute cases (animals in need of sudden or emergency care).
- Consulting with patients who are affected by chronic (longer-term or gradual) conditions.
- Checking that the animals I've seen before and operated on are improving over time.
- Carrying out surgery.
- Preparing lectures for conferences or training courses.
- Writing papers for academic journals and books – just like this one!
- Managing the practice with my management colleagues.
- Working with charity.
- Making my TV show.

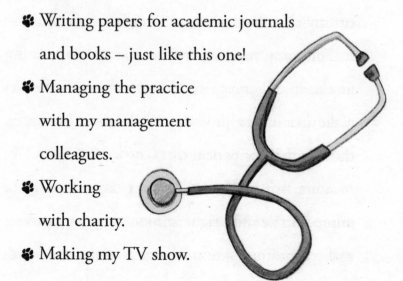

These things often happen at the same time – such as operating and making my TV show. Every day is busy and varied! But it's probably the surgery that I'm best known for. We have several specialist surgeons at Fitzpatrick Referrals, but we only operate on animals with problems affecting the skeleton – that's orthopaedics – or problems affecting the brain, spinal cord and nerves – that's neurosurgery. I call surgery 'cutting', because it involves the use of a scalpel, which is a small and extremely sharp bladed instrument (trust me, I've cut myself enough times to know!).

For many years I've further specialised in using implants and prostheses (artificial body parts) to make an animal's life better. You'll learn more about those in the stories of this book.

Some surgeries are quick, but others are unpredictable and can take many hours. It's gruelling and exhausting work, needing constant focus, leaning over the operating table. I've got a bad back as a result, as well as plenty of other aches and pains.

Before I begin any operation, I need to prepare in just the same way as a surgeon for human patients. **One of the most important things is cleanliness, because I don't want to cause an infection.**

- I wear a surgical head covering so that nothing can fall from my hair on to a patient, and a surgical mask so that I don't breathe where I'm operating.
- I sometimes wear an eye visor if things are going to get really messy.
- I use an anti-microbial soap to clean my hands, fingers and forearms, and I regularly trim my nails.
- I use a special hand-sterilising solution for ninety seconds.
- A theatre veterinary care assistant helps me put on a sterile surgical gown and gloves.

🐾 Everything I touch after that is sterilised, so that the surgical equipment has been thoroughly cleaned of micro-organisms to reduce the chance of infection.

The patient is unconscious before I begin thanks to anaesthesia, and the area we're operating on has been shaved and sterilised too. I place drapes (paper or plastic coverings) over the spot. All the sterilised tools I need, as well as any implants or screws, will be on a tray or two nearby. We might have scans on the display too, so I can remind myself exactly what to expect when we get inside.

Some of the surgeries I've carried out hundreds of times. I often perform hip replacements, and I can get from first incision (a precise cut with my scalpel) to final stitches in less than an hour. When I perform spinal surgery to remove material that has exploded from a dried-out disc and is squashing the spinal cord, that rarely takes longer than fifteen to thirty minutes. But other operations can take far longer when unexpected complications occur. The longest I've ever been standing beside the operation table is **over twelve hours**! It's also important to realise that though experience helps reduce surgical time, doing a good job is always more important than how long it takes the surgeon to complete the task.

The tools of my trade are basic in some ways – the same sorts of things a surgeon has been using for centuries: hooks to move organs aside, forceps to grip, a saw for cutting bone (though mine is an air-driven micro-saw) and a special needle holder to stitch up. The design of these tools has been perfected over many years, and the materials are modern. I use a drill to implant screws, and a suction tube to take blood away from the site of the operation. A cauteriser can seal stubborn blood vessels.

During an operation, there are usually only three or four people involved: me, an intern to hold the limb, the anaesthetic nurse and a theatre veterinary care assistant to hand me things. And the patient, of course. We work with few words. I do say 'please' and 'thank you' a lot in surgery but during the challenging bits especially, there's not a lot of talking. Whatever doesn't help the animal isn't important.

During times when my TV show, *The Supervet*, is being filmed, there might well be a member of the TV crew dressed in sterile kit attending the surgery as well. It might seem strange to some, but I'm used to the cameras now. When I'm operating, I talk to the camera as I would to a friend, explaining what I'm doing. All my focus is on the animal on the table in front of me.

The Road to Recovery

After I operate on a patient and they're stitched up, he or she is moved to the wards to recover. There are separate wards for dogs and cats, and each animal has their own compartment where they can rest in a safe and warm place. We have a no-bars policy in my practice, so the compartments are made of special reinforced glass and the patient doesn't feel caged in. We sometimes even have a radio and TV for them too. A theatre nurse is in charge of helping the patient wake up again and then the ward nurses and veterinary care assistants take over, giving medicines, measuring out food and looking after pees and poos!

Depending on how serious the operation was, recovery can take from days, even weeks, to months. Animals aren't like humans – you can't tell them to put their feet up! They often don't know what's good for them, so stopping them from moving about is pretty much impossible. After an orthopaedic operation, dogs and cats can be their own worst enemies. When they see their human families again for the first time, dogs might wag their bums like crazy and just want to jump, and cats may feel like they want to run around!

For a bone or joint to heal after being put back together, the last thing I want is the patient upsetting the repair. I always say, 'No running, jumping, slipping or sliding.' I also say, 'No licking!' whenever there's a surgical wound. When I use a metal scaffold or frame (which is called an **'external skeletal fixator'** or **'ESF'** for short) on the outside of a limb to hold bone pieces in place, it's critical that my patient doesn't chew this. So we use various devices, such as an inflatable tube on a dog's neck to stop them from turning to chew, or a cone to stop them from licking the wound or the apparatus.

Some people call it the 'cone of shame' but I prefer the 'cone of courage'!

The same goes for bandages. A dog or cat's teeth can easily take off coverings or bandages and get to metal staples or nylon stitches pretty much anywhere on their body! So the cone of courage is the only option for many.

Once, I hurt my neck badly and had to wear a brace. I wore it for several weeks, with strict instruction from my doctor not to do anything silly. **The cones I put on the necks of dogs and cats are to stop them from bothering their stitches or dressings**, but my collar was there to keep me from making any sudden movements since I had broken one of the bones in my neck. I empathised greatly with my patients – who actually taught me patience. It was itchy and frustrating at times – just as it no doubt is for them – and, like them too, I was so grateful when I was finally able to remove it! Animals and humans have way more in common than we often care to admit.

Infection is always a worry after an operation.

It generally happens when a tiny bacterial micro-organism gets into a surgical site or a wound and multiplies. Bacteria are living things too – they have a drive to survive just like us and the animals in our care! Even with all the sterilising and self-cleaning we do before and during a procedure, sometimes infection can happen. It could get in during the surgery, but with all the precautions, it certainly shouldn't.

Usually, an infection either comes from somewhere else in the animal – like the mouth, guts or urinary bladder (the organ that holds our wee) through the bloodstream or from the environment, such as a dog licking a wound or from a bed they may lie on. Infection can make an animal very poorly, can result in tissue destruction (destroying the normal appearance and function of that tissue) that is so bad we need to consider full limb amputation (cutting off a leg), or can even cause death if it spreads, which is called sepsis. We give medicines called antibiotics to fight infection, and everyone who works on the wards is trained to spot any signs very early. We do this by observing the recovering patients carefully, keeping an eye on wounds to look out for any **pus** (horrible yellow oozing liquid!), seeing their behaviour, how they move, what their appetite is like and measuring their temperatures regularly.

When it is time for the animal to go home, I talk to their guardians about the recovery process, including how much exercise an animal can get, what they should eat, problems to look out for and when to come back for a check-up. I tell them to call any time if they have concerns. **Surgery isn't just about the animal — it's a worrying time for everyone who loves that animal too.**

When my patients come back to me for a check-up, I want to see that the healing process is going well and that the body part I have operated is improving, and make sure there's no infection.

Human guardians often know their companion animals best and can let you know if they're out of sorts or back to normal. You can tell a lot just from the way a dog or cat behaves – if a tail is wagging and his or her eyes are bright, that's a good sign!

I'll also change any bandages and clean up wounds or remove stitches. We take repeat X-ray images and/or CT scans at regular intervals for follow-up too.

After their surgeries, animals who come to Fitzpatrick Referrals sometimes have to learn to walk again on three legs or to live with an implant, a new piece of spinal column or a replaced or fused joint. It's important to do this as safely as possible, and that's where hydrotherapy and physiotherapy come in (see pages 83 and 84).

Being a vet or vet nurse are dream jobs for many. If you want to become either, you need to work hard at school. You need top marks to get into vet school; it's a long period of training and there are dozens of different areas you can go into afterwards (see page 80). The most important thing, though, isn't passing exams or getting certificates – it's trying to always do the right thing for the animals in your care and being compassionate and caring. I would hire someone for the size of their heart over their exam results any day – but you do need the knowledge too.

Saying Goodbye

Sadly, sometimes an animal's quality of life is so poor that it's not fair to carry on and it's kinder to let them pass peacefully away. This can be after a brief or long illness, or after trying with surgery that didn't work out. It is important to always do the right thing for the animal, no matter how hard it may be for us as their guardians. I find that families just want the peace of mind of knowing they have done their best for their friend.

Euthanasia is ending an animal's life to relieve suffering, and it's by far the hardest part of my job. It is advised when we decide an animal is in too much pain or can't be made better. In such cases, we talk to the animal's human companions and explain that we think the kindest thing to do would be to put their animal friend to sleep permanently.

People saying goodbye to the animal they love is the saddest part of my job and it never gets easier. For most people, their animal companion is part of their family and they share many happy memories. When the time comes to perform euthanasia, we try to make things as quiet and comfortable as possible. Usually, the families want to be there, and I do advise this for most, as it brings most peace for the final farewell. I always give them some private moments afterwards with their loved one. It's truly a privilege to share this planet with animals that share their love with us unconditionally.

What About the Money?

I remember my daddy visiting me twice in my life when I was working as a vet. The first time, I was operating in a garden hut beside a house. We took X-ray images, prepared the patients and the kit and operated all in the same room. The drill I used back then for placing screws was the same as a builder's and the drill I used for spinal surgery was that of a carpenter, both wrapped in sterile drapes. I was excited to show him how far I'd come since working on the farm with him, even with my basic tools.

The second time he visited wasn't that long before he passed away. I had just started building Fitzpatrick Referrals. I showed him the foundations for a hydrotherapy pool in a building that was converted from an old hay barn similar to the one we had back on the farm in Ireland. Even though he was amazed that we provided such facilities for recovery from surgery, he just nodded and gave me the same advice he had done when I was a teenager: 'Be careful with the pennies, and the pounds will take care of themselves. All dreams need bravery and persistence and many of them need money too.' In other words, he advised that I be careful about running out of money. He was right. Soon afterwards, I ran out of money and Fitzpatrick Referrals might not have come into existence at all if it hadn't been for bravery and persistence.

My profession today is very different to how it was when I graduated, and this isn't just because technology and knowledge has improved – but also because veterinary medicine has become a big business. This sadly means that the type of care an animal may get, and who provides that care, may not always be in the best interest of the patient and their family. Vets are often limited with the treatments they can offer, even when it might be best for the animal. In my opinion, sometimes practices might offer surgeries that their well-meaning clinical team don't have enough training on too.

This worries me a great deal. A veterinary practice does need to make enough money to keep going and pay everyone's wages, but making money should never be the primary goal of being a vet and caring for animals. I insist on offering all of the options to all of my patients all of the time, even if that involves sending that patient elsewhere because my practice isn't the best in that particular area of expertise. When I see patients today, I do my best by each and every one of them. My practice is 'independent', which means it is not owned by a big business that must make lots of money for its shareholders (these are people who all own part of the business). Sometimes, with the more complex operations, by the time myself and my team have done all the engineering planning, implant manufacture, surgery and aftercare, we've made very little profit. I could make much more money with simple, quick surgeries. But I believe that the best care for the animals and their families who come to see me is more important than all the money in the world. If you decide to become a vet, I hope that is something you will take with you too.

It's also important to remember that **things don't always go to plan, and that's OK.** My big dream was to build the four pillars of surgery – orthopaedics, neurosurgery, soft tissue surgery and cancer, which meant borrowing even more money to build a second hospital. But sadly, this didn't work out – we all worked hard, but some of my surgeon colleagues left, others wanted to do things differently and eventually, I ran out of money. I learned that there are more important things than money when chasing your dreams, such as: **being resilient** learning from what's gone wrong, continuing to do your best for the animals with whatever resources you do have and retaining high levels of compassion and care. I also learned that everybody's dreams are different and if you're playing on a team, as you always are in veterinary practice, **then everyone needs to work together**. All anyone can do is be true to their own dreams, whatever they may be. And, as Daddy wisely said: '**Even if you don't have money, bravery and persistence can still keep your dream alive.**'

CHAPTER 5
Prostheses, Implants and Bionic Legs

At Fitzpatrick Referrals, most of our work is neuro-orthopaedics – that means helping animals with their mobility (movement). Their problems can be horribly traumatic and bloody (in the case of traffic accidents) or invisible to the naked eye (genetic conditions affecting their joints or spine, for example). Most of the time, operations involve moving or removing bone, treating inflamed joints, repairing broken bones or operating on spinal discs. But I am probably best known for my work with customised implants and prostheses.

Prostheses – artificial body parts – have been

used to help humans for thousands of years, either for cosmetic (appearance) purposes or to make life easier by aiding mobility.

Back in the time when war was common and surgery was limited, a soldier returning from battle might have asked for a fake nose or eye to replace one that had been chopped off or damaged, or a wooden lower leg may have allowed them to walk again.

I remember the first time I saw a prosthetic leg. It was my Uncle Paul. I knew he'd lost the bottom part of his leg in a motorbike accident as a young man. He walked with a bad limp. But he never wore shorts, so I'd never seen where his leg ended and the artificial part of his leg, which was made mostly of wood, began. We were out one hot day fishing together on the River Shannon in Ireland and he was rather grumpy. As I rowed the boat, he pulled up his trouser leg and I saw it for the first time – a wooden leg fastened with straps to his upper leg. Sweating and grumbling and wincing with pain, he unfastened the straps. Without warning me, he pulled the prosthetic away. I'm sorry to say I

screamed!

The stump, where it joined the socket of the artificial leg, was sore and scabby, like a piece of meat. I was so shocked that I jolted back suddenly, the boat tipped and his wooden leg went over the side! (Don't worry, we recovered it later, further downstream).

TYPES OF LIMB PROSTHESIS

Most people think of a 'prosthesis' as just an artificial object attached to the stump left behind after someone has lost part of their arm or leg. But technically speaking, a prosthesis is a device used to replace or add to a missing or impaired part of the body. In this way, some of the implants that I place inside the body can be called prostheses too – for example if it's a large chunk of metal replacing a removed bit of cancerous bone or implant components that replace a joint – then those implants can be called prostheses. There are broadly three kinds of limb prostheses:

1. Metal, plastic or other material placed inside the limb to replace a part of the skeleton. This could involve replacing bone destroyed by an injury or by cancer, or replacing the joints of limbs, for example.

2. Metal attached to the bones where a hand or foot is missing in a human or any of the four feet are missing in a cat or dog. This implant can be a metal rod inserted inside the bones or attached by plates and screws outside the bones. The skin joins to mesh on the metal where it comes out of the bone and a peg known as a 'spigot' pokes out from the skin. We then attach the external foot on to this

peg. So a so-called 'bionic leg' has both an inner and an outer part. This works a lot like a deer's antler, where bone grows from nubs on their skulls, through the velvety skin without getting infected.

3. A socket made out of various kinds of plastic or fiberglass and a pressure-absorbing cushion which is placed directly on to the stump left behind after part of the limb is lost. For my Uncle Paul and other humans years ago, this was mainly built of wood beneath which was a metal leg and foot or arm and hand. In animals, the socket, which is often made out of fiberglass, can extend to a rubber sole. This is called a stump-socket prosthesis and is the most common kind of limb replacement for both humans and animals. This is not a bionic limb, since it is not directly attached to the skeleton.

In both human and animal surgery nowadays, plastic and metal joints are common for hip and knee replacements, and man-made discs can replace worn-out parts of the spinal column. These are all prostheses inside the body. Modern advancements in medical prosthetic implants are making all sorts of things possible. For example, **a lost eyeball might be replaced by what is sometimes known as a 'glass eye'**, but is actually made out of hard plastic acrylic. And more recently, there are electronic prosthetic implants to make the blind see and the deaf hear! The future will bring us even more miracles with prosthetic implants to replace tissues of all kinds.

It's only in the last few decades that we've started to apply the same level of care to the animals in our lives as we might expect for ourselves. When I started trying to help animals with prostheses of any kind, I was often looking to the world of human medicine and work that had been done by using experimental animals to test implants for humans, and now our facilities at Fitzpatrick Referrals rival any human hospital in the world. Dogs and cats have been losing legs to accidents and illness forever. If the same accident doesn't kill them and an amputation is reasonable, both cats and dogs can walk, run and jump quite well with three remaining limbs. I'll often say this to my patients' human companions. It may not be advisable or even possible to replace a limb with an implant or prosthesis in many cases. Animals are incredibly resilient.

Losing two limbs is much more impactful on a pet cat or dog. Sadly, an accident I see frequently is when an animal has been hit by a car and dragged beneath it or trapped under a wheel. In this case, two legs could be badly damaged. In cases where the bottom part of the legs can't be saved, partial amputation or euthanasia may both be reasonable options. Many vets recommend euthanasia, but with the advances in implant technology, it's now possible to give the poor animal a new lease of life using the prostheses I've described. I was the first person in the world to use this technology successfully in dogs and cats!

Some families of dogs who have lost part of both hind legs or who have lost control of them due to a spinal injury may also opt for a mobility cart with wheels. This isn't a prosthesis, but for some families it can provide a good quality of life for their canine friend. Cats, however, generally don't take to these kinds of mobility trolleys very well.

Peanut and Oscar, the Bionic Cats

Cats tend to be more independent than dogs. Unlike dogs, who may be happy to remain near their human family, **most cats like some time alone**. Many cats are natural roamers – as darkness falls, their human companions let them out to explore and even secretly hunt. Most times they're back in the morning, hungry and ready for a cuddle.

But their wandering can lead to problems. Over six hundred cats are hit by cars every single day in the UK and as traffic increases, so does that awful number. Cats are also prone to getting themselves trapped in garages or sheds and having scraps with other cats. If you live with a cat, and he or she ventures outside, there's a chance at some point you'll be sitting in a primary care vet practice with your furry friend suffering from their night-time adventures.

But the cats referred to me are beyond the help of a primary care vet.

Oscar, a black shorthair cat, had been through a horrific accident. He lived in the countryside and liked to explore the maize fields behind his house, no doubt in search of scurrying field mice or rabbits. Unfortunately, he met a combine harvester. It's not hard to understand how it happened. In the high maize, he wouldn't have known which direction the machine was coming from, and the noise of the growling engine and shaking ground would have startled him. He ran the wrong way and his two hind paws were caught in the harvester's blades and completely severed.

When Oscar's family brought him to see me, he'd already been looked after by a primary care vet, who'd bandaged his stumps and given him antibiotics to try to prevent infection. But this was only a temporary measure. Both of his hind feet had been cut off below his ankle joints. In cats the ankle is the joint between the **tibia** (shin bone) and the **talus** and **calcaneus** (the two main moving bones). **Cats stand on their tippy-toes so that the metatarsus (the arch of the foot) is off the ground.** But Oscar's feet arches and toes were chopped off, and only the two main moving bones remained.

I'd fitted prosthetic implants to one leg before but, to my knowledge, no one had ever fitted two at the same time, and definitely not also keeping the moving ankle joints. Oscar was only two years old, with a possibly long life ahead, so his family asked me to try. To do this operation:

1. I attached an implant as a rod into the calcaneus (the bigger ankle bone) and fused it to the talus (the smaller ankle bone) in each of Oscar's hind legs. The bone then could grow on to the metal rod and the skin would grow around a specialised dome of metal in the shape of a honeycomb at the base of the rod. This was the inner part of the bionic leg, technically called an endoprosthesis.

2. Then I attached a rigid blade to the spigot that poked out of each hind leg, which acted as feet. These are technically called exoprostheses.

Cat ankle bones are tiny, so I had to be very careful with the drilling and implantation. Thankfully the surgery went well, and before long, Oscar was able to run around happily on his two new bionic hind feet!

Peanut was all black, with a white muzzle and chest. He came to us by quite a different route, but the operation we performed was similar. Peanut had been born to a feral cat (one that lives in the wild without a human guardian). But Peanut had a genetic deformity meaning his front legs were bent inwards, and so he walked on his carpi (his wrist joints) rather than his paws. He was born somewhere outdoors, but when his mother had to move on with her kittens, she abandoned little Peanut, who couldn't keep up. Luckily, he was rescued by a kind human companion, Denise, who brought him into her home to live with her other cats.

Peanut was eighteen months old when I met him, and he was clearly a fighter, getting on with life despite his difficulties. It constantly amazes me how tough and determined animals can be, even when they're suffering and the odds are stacked against them. Peanut was doing his best to live life like any other cat – hunting and exploring in the land around Denise's house. But his deformity was causing problems, because as he jumped around on the rocks and in the woodland, he was tearing up the soft skin of his knuckled-over wrists. He couldn't feel his paws when they were touched because the nerve endings hadn't developed properly. Denise had to **apply fresh bandages every day** to his wounds. Without help with walking, infection was becoming a greater and greater issue for Peanut's front legs and his quality of life would soon become unsustainable, so he would end up being put to sleep. He had the added complication of deformity of his elbows, which was getting worse the longer he struggled on his wrists. Something had to be done. Removing his front

paws was the first step of the operation, but given that he'd never used them anyway, he wouldn't miss them.

The sort of implants I used on both Peanut and Oscar are made to measure from a metal called **titanium**. It's perfect because it's strong, light and is 'bio-compatible', meaning that once inside the body, it bonds well to tissue and doesn't cause a reaction. **The implants were 3D-printed,** just another of the incredible scientific advances of recent years, then finished by hand. In fact, even between Oscar's operation in 2009 and Peanut's in 2016, design technology had significantly improved. Oscar's hind feet were like blades and Peanuts front feet were like pogo sticks. Both are still alive at time I'm writing this book and got on with life as if nothing had happened. Whenever they wore out their bionic feet, it was relatively easy to change them for new ones.

Betsy and Her Skateboard Wheel

Road accidents cause many of the traumatic injuries I see at the practice. There are so many vehicles on the roads, and cats especially like to roam at night. But dogs can have accidents too – getting startled by traffic and running into the road. Betsy the black cockapoo was very young when she was hit by a car, damaging the nerves in her right front leg and leaving it partially paralysed. She was dragging her paw, hopping around on her remaining three legs. Her family were still hoping for the best, when the bottom part of her leg became gangrenous, which occurs when the blood supply can't reach the tissue and it dies. There was no choice but to amputate Betsy's paw. But she was only six months old at the time and her family asked me if we *had* to remove all of her leg or if we could we do anything to improve her quality of life by only removing part of it and using a prosthetic. Just like with Peanut and Oscar, the answer was yes!

The prosthetic implant I use has a very long name – a PerFiTS (Percutaneous Fixation To the Skeleton).

This is anchored to the skeleton using a combination of a peg, plates and screws. An external prosthesis can then be attached to it. We've been developing and advancing the technology for over a decade, and the clever part of the newest design is that it has metal mesh for skin and bone to grow on to, so the prosthesis becomes part of the animal's own body. The internal part is an endoprosthesis (endo means 'inside') and this is attached to an exoprosthesis (a prosthesis outside the body). In Betsy's case, at first we tried an aluminium blade and a foot made from the rubber of a bicycle tyre – but she was so active that she kept wearing it out! So we designed and made a new foot for her out of a skateboard wheel. As you'll discover later in this book, we can get very creative when it comes to making prostheses.

Prostheses and implants are nothing new in human or animal surgery, but the technology is improving all the time. For many years, implant surgery has been tested on animals before being performed on humans according to regulations, and sadly, this involves animals dying in the process.

Now, thankfully, there are often times where we can design implants with computer simulations based on previous cases, so we may not have to test on as many animals in the same way in the future. But there is still more we can do. For example, we could learn from animals who have implants that really need them, rather than only experimenting on otherwise healthy animals to achieve safe implants for humans. I am very passionate about human and animal doctors sharing their learnings, innovation and new ideas, so that we can give all patients – human and animal – the best quality of life possible.

CHAPTER 6
Superhero Pets

When I'm designing a prosthetic or an implant to fix a problem, I often turn back to the comic books I read as a boy and the characters with superhuman gifts and abilities who fought crime, helped people and saved the world. Those comic book heroes who kept me enthralled and entertained in my bedroom have helped me create hundreds of modern-day superhero pets at the practice. As a child I was fascinated by Wolverine because he had a metal endoskeleton made from a fictional metal called adamantium (which was actually fused to the bones of his skeleton). I thought that if I could build a metal endoskeleton, then that would be far better for fixing bones than the twigs and twine that my father used to splint the legs of lambs. Wolverine's adamantium claws turned out to be just the right fit for a special canine friend called Winston.

Wolverine Winston

Winston was still a puppy when his distraught dad brought him in. Just five months old, he was a cuddly white Staffordshire Bull Terrier cross-breed. But the little dog was in a terrible state: his front feet had been caught under the wheels of a car and the wounds were severe. Both of his front paws were almost completely severed.

I've been presented with dozens of similar injuries in my time, but it doesn't get any easier to see an animal – and their human companion – in distress. In emergency situations like this, it's important to keep calm and thinking clearly. Shock and blood loss can kill. And there are many factors to be weighed up. In the past, a vet would simply have put such an animal to sleep without question. And I have to say, with Winston, I definitely considered it and gave his family that option. On my TV show, I try to show this reality. Not all animals can be saved, however much we want them to be. Sometimes it may be the kindest option to allow them to pass away peacefully.

We make an oath when we begin our work as vets:

Above all, that my constant endeavour will be to ensure the health and welfare of animals committed to my care.

What seems an easy promise is anything but simple sometimes. What are 'health' and 'welfare'? Those words mean different things to different people. For some, they may think that even if an operation is possible, it might involve too much for them and the animal to go through. As I've explained, 'the right thing to do' in ethical terms is different for everyone. In this case, an animal's guardian has to make a tough decision, and vets disagree about what might be the 'best' pathway.

My initial reaction when I saw Winston's awful state, having given him medicine to ease his pain, was that I didn't know if his front paws could be reattached. The damage to the muscles, the blood vessels and the bone was severe. This was indeed awful, but his young age was in his favour. This meant that if I could work out a way to save his front paws without putting him through what might be considered 'too much', then there was a chance of good healing and a long life ahead. Had he been twelve years old, for example, I would have thought differently, because he wouldn't have had a whole life ahead of him and the period of recovery could have been longer. **Young dogs generally heal quicker than older dogs.**

Still, the operation would be a long one. And – it's important to say – expensive. An operation can take most of a day and involve ten or twelve people, all of whom need to be paid. The equipment used is often costly too. Another promise we make as vets is to be completely open with a pet's human companion about the pros and cons, costs, risks and potential benefits of any procedure. It's also important to tell them that they can also choose which surgeon they wish to have operate on their best friend. I went over all this with Winston's family and I made sure to emphasise that there was no judgement from me if they'd asked me to give him a lethal injection then and there, allowing him to pass away peacefully in their arms.

Of course, Winston himself had no say in the matter. Or at least no human words left his mouth. This is similar to a human doctor talking to the parents of a baby who is poorly and cannot speak for themselves. **My main concern is always the animals. We know that animals feel emotions – happiness and sadness, anxiety and excitement – and they respond to emotions in their human companions, too.** This is called 'sentience'. Did Winston understand any of our discussions? Did he have any sense of what his injuries meant or was he just confused and in pain? All of us have a desire to live, and in his puppy eyes I saw this clearly. Other vets may have seen things differently and there's no judgement from me there either.

In the end, the family decided they wanted to try to save Winston's life. We'd found a way to help through charitable donations from others. The first steps were to make Winston as comfortable as possible, support what was left of his bone structure and try to prevent infection. I built an ESF (see page 109), where pins were placed in the bigger bones and wires in the smaller bones from the outside, above and below the damaged bones. I attached the pins and wires to a metal frame on each of his front legs to support his front paws. I managed to prevent any infection, but paws usually have bones, and there were no **metacarpal bones** (palm bones) in one of his paws – a gap that was never going to 'fill in' on its own. As if that wasn't enough, the carpal bones (wrist bones) on both sides had also been sheared off on the road. Winston was also having trouble walking because what was left of his toes couldn't bear his bodyweight.

I was at a dead end. Any treatment now would be untested waters. As so often before, I found inspiration in human medicine. Specifically, the work done by a Russian surgeon called Gavriil Abramovich Ilizarov. He'd operated on injured soldiers after the Second World War by attaching spaced metal rings to damaged bone with metal wires (which originally were recycled spokes from the wheels of bicycles!). The rings were attached above and below the damaged bit, so that the bone formed the centre of the ring. In this way the pieces of bone were suspended like one of those bridges you see with long wires. Ilizarov discovered that by moving the wire rings away from each other in a certain way, you could actually encourage the bone to grow, which is called osteogenesis.

The challenges in Winston's case were that there was too much bone torn away from one of his palms and both wrists were missing a lot of bone too.

Wolverine could release three sharp metal prongs from the knuckles of his hands. I wondered if I might be able to use such metal prongs to make new palm bones for Winston's right front paw. But where could I get new bone that might be the same shape and size as the palm bones? Then I had a 'eureka' moment! Winston had a lovely long tail. I thought that if I amputated (cut off) his tail, I could take the **vertebrae** (the small spinal bones that make up the tail) from it and stack them in pairs along wire prongs inside the paw. Each pair of vertebrae would be just the right shape, size and length to reconstruct one metacarpal bone of the four bones in the palm of Winston's paw.

I needed to hold these in place and encourage the bone to grow, so I took inspiration from Dr Ilizarov again! Here's what I did . . .

1. I lined up the tail vertebrae in pairs end to end along four wire prongs for Winston's right front paw.

2. Then I built circular metal frames using aluminium rings, like two bicycle wheels placed beside each other, with the bones as the hub and wires as spokes piercing through the bones. The two

'Wolverine wires' which skewer through each pair of stacked tail vertebrae, holding them in place

rings were linked on the outside of the paw by threaded rods.

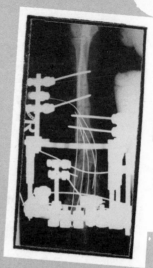

3. I attached one ring to the bottom part of Winston's forearm and the other to the toes of the front paw at right angles to the vertebrae prong wires.

4. The two ring-wheels were moved alternatively toward and away from each other by a tiny amount a few times a day. We did this by using a device similar to an extendible telescope on the threads of the rods that connected the rings. This helped blood pump through the transplanted vertebrae bones, gradually forming new palm bones for Winston!

5. I also took a small block of bone from his pelvis to make this repair stronger.

6. I drilled out all of the remaining cartilage tissue that coated the carpal bones in the wrists.

7. I fused all these carpal bones together with the metacarpal palm bones and the radius and ulna

bones of the forearms using marrow bone (this is the soft spongy insides of some bones) taken from his pelvis. Amazingly, marrow cells can grow into new bone, and it doesn't end there! They can also work as a scaffolding mesh, so that cells from nearby bones can grow and create new bone, like a trellis in a garden that supports growing plants.

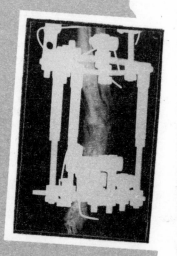

8. For Winston's left wrist and front paw, I used a simpler frame that just needed to fuse the wrist solid with bone marrow. Then Winston walked around on the two frames while the 'biological miracle' took place.

But while I was trying to get the bone to grow, there was another problem to deal with: the tendons and skin had been ripped off the front of one of the paws as well as the palm bones! I tried to think creatively again so:

1. I reorganized the external frame on the right front paw so that the transplanted tail vertebrae could now become solid metacarpal (palm) bones. I then attached another pair of extendable rods to this new frame at a specific angle.

2. I linked an arch to the ends of these rods, which acted as an anchor for thick nylon fishing line. I threaded the nylon through the edge of the skin at the gap, protected by some plastic tubing, so it wouldn't slice through the fragile skin.

3. By making these rods longer by a tiny amount every day, I slowly stretched the skin edge using the nylon fishing line anchor and closed the gap, like gradually pulling a blanket up over a bed. I kept the tissue beneath moisturised with a special gel throughout.

Nylon fishing line anchored to the skin edge using plastic tubing, which pulls the skin across like a blanket when the rods are lengthened

With any surgery, there's a chance of failure. I have failed many times in my career as a surgeon and it's sadly true that when you need to innovate to solve a difficult challenge, you can often come under criticism when it doesn't go to plan. That's just human nature. I'd been honest with Winston's guardians from the start that the treatment might not work. But to the delight of everyone, especially Winston, the transplanted bones and marrow grew into new palm bones and fused the wrists solid with the forelimbs on both sides. Just like the comic-book character Wolverine, with his amazing self-healing powers, Winston's body grew stronger each day. He had a long road to recovery, but on the day we took him outside and watched him run on the grass beside the practice, we all knew we'd made the right decision. Winston went on to live a happy life, even without his tail! No tail, but a tale to tell!

Winston was the first, but over the years I honed the 'Wolverine technique' through experience with several other patients in similar difficult situations.

Miracle Milly

Milly came to see me almost a decade after Winston. She was a very special puppy, a black Labrador, full of energy. She was also best friend to a teenage girl called Jess. The bond they had reminded me of that I'd shared with Pirate as a boy, because she had had difficult times, as I had, and Milly had been her companion through it all. I think some animals and people are meant to be together, and these two were living proof.

Jess had always loved animals. When she was younger, she'd had cats, hamsters, rabbits and chickens, but Milly was the love of her life. It was Jess who first noticed that something was wrong with Milly's front paws, and her vet explained what was happening. The poor dog had a very serious degenerative disease in the knuckles of both front paws, which are technically called **metacarpo-phalangeal joints**. This meant her toes were separating from her knuckles and literally falling off. The effect was that the metacarpal bones (the palm bones between the wrist and the fingers, as for Winston) were pressing down like hammers on to her pads, splitting open the skin and causing severe infection. She had tried different protective boots, **but none of them had worked**.

Jess's mum had been advised that putting Milly to sleep to ease her suffering might be the kindest option, and we were her last chance.

As with Winston, I thought Wolverine could come to the rescue again, but this time the operation had an added evolutionary component:

1. First, I used wires like Wolverine's prongs to skewer the knuckle joints solid once I had drilled away any remaining cartilage.

2. As for Winston's wrist joints, I grafted marrow bone (this time taken from near the shoulders) to get these joints to fuse solid.

3. Milly couldn't walk on her toes as they were too fragile, so I built an ESF scaffold with aluminium rings, just as I had for Winston, and added arches under her feet, so that they were raised up like horseshoes that she could walk on.

4. I attached all the rings to a rod and pins in the radius and ulna bones up along both of her forearms to temporarily bridge her wrists. This was a new version of the frame, which I called PAWS (Pedal Arch Wire Scaffold). Actually you've already seen a picture of a PAWS frame in the X-ray image on page 9. Here's a CT scan.

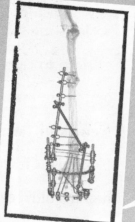

The operation was a success! Like Winston, Milly had a long road to recovery, but with Jess at her side, she did amazingly well. Her frames came off just before Christmas, and it was best present anyone could have asked for. Milly really was a Christmas miracle.

New Bone for an Actual Superhero

Hero the German Shepherd cross was only four months old. He loved playing with his puppy pals in the park, but wasn't watching where he was going. That's how he ran headlong into a bicycle. At first, his family wasn't too worried about his front left leg limp. They thought he might have some bruising or a sprain, but it didn't go away. In fact, it got worse, and soon he didn't want to put any weight on the foot at all. The limb had developed a curve and looked shorter than his right leg. His paw began to point outwards. His family was very worried and because his love and joy had been helping them through a very tough time, they told me that he really was their superhero (which is how he got his name!).

At the practice, we took X-ray images and CT scans and diagnosed the problem to be damaged 'growth plates' (the medical term is 'physes') at the ends of his two forearm bones, the ulna and the radius. These are areas at the ends of long bones where a layer of cartilage cells in a newborn baby or animal becomes bone as they quite literally 'grow up'. But Hero's forearm bones were not growing at the same speed, which caused the leg to bend. This is called the 'bowstring effect', because the shorter ulna is like a string and the radius curves like a bow.

Even more importantly though for Hero, the growth plate at the bottom of the radius bone wasn't growing anywhere near as quickly as it should have been either. This meant his left forearm was four centimeters shorter than his right forearm when I first met him and his situation was getting worse daily because his right leg continued to grow.

His options were to leave him as he was, in which case he would never bear weight on his short and deformed limb again, amputate his left front leg entirely, leaving him on three legs, make his leg longer with a prosthetic or to try to fix the situation.

Straightening limbs is something that I do all the time, nowadays often using custom-made cutting guides and special plates all designed on a computer. But it is actually possible to lengthen bones as well. This is done by cutting the bone in a special way and then gradually pulling the opposite ends apart. If this is performed at the right speed, over the correct amount of time, new bone cells grow in the gap between the bone sections. This is a process called 'distraction osteogenesis' – a fancy name meaning 'making bone by pulling apart' and it was discovered by the surgeon Ilizarov, who I mentioned earlier.

So, let's get technical again. In Hero's case, I did as follows:

1. I made cuts in his radius and ulna forearm bones.
2. Then I anchored aluminum rings to both the top and bottom parts using wires like the spokes of a miniature bicycle wheel with the bone at the center, as for Winston and Milly.
3. I twisted the top and bottom rings in such a way that the radius and ulna bones were straightened again. I joined them together with three threaded rods, as for Winston.
4. The challenge of growing his forearm remained. That's where the wonderful biological miracle of distraction osteogenesis comes in. Like Winston, each of the threaded rods were

mounted within a shaft like an extendable telescope. I could extend the three telescopes by a quarter or a half a millimeter using a dial on each shaft, so pulling the bones apart a little at a time.

5. I would do this four times a day. As the bone gap widened, the bone cells, which are called 'osteoblasts', were stimulated by movement to produce new bone.

6. On an X-ray image this looked like those streaky clouds you sometimes see in the sky, but gradually these growing bone cells became solid bone. With daily physiotherapy, Hero's muscles and tendons stretched alongside the bones.

After four months in total, Hero could run around and enjoy a rough-and-tumble lifestyle once more, now carefully avoiding bicycles. It was more than a little strange that a bicycle wheel got Hero into bother in the first place and then miniature bicycle wheels on a frame got him out of bother.

Captain America to the Rescue

While Wolverine is known for his razor-sharp claws of adamantium, Captain America is known for his indestructible shield of vibranium. But it isn't only superheroes who need a shield to protect them. Sometimes animals do too! I'm going to tell you about a dog called Roger, who had a problem with his spine.

THE SPINE

The spine is what holds life together. It's made up of bones called vertebrae. I tell my patients to think of the spine like a train, and the vertebrae as carriages. Between them are discs, made of a tough tissue called cartilage. Each disc is like a jam doughnut where the dough on the outside is the dense cartilage ring and the jam on the inside is the 'nucleus pulposus'. These discs are like the buffers between train carriages when they shunt against each other. They absorb shock and they are joints as well, allowing the spine to bend in multiple directions.

The spine is so important because the vertebrae stacked end-to-end have a canal inside them so the delicate spinal cord can pass through each one and is protected from the neck right down to the bottom. The spinal cord carries nerve signals from the brain to the rest of the body. It allows us to feel where our limbs are, and move our hands and feet. Because of my work, I see spinal problems often. All mammals, as well as birds, fish, reptiles and amphibians, are vertebrates (animals with spinal columns).

If the spine gets damaged, it can cause all sorts of painful issues – but particularly it interferes with the nerve signals. Sometimes the damage might be a break caused by an accident, general wear and tear or something the animal is born with that develops over time, which is called a developmental condition. Canines in the wild, like wolves, tend to live around eight years on average, before injury, harsh habitats or periods of scarce food make it hard to thrive. But our animal companions live a life of relative luxury with vaccinations, nutritious diets and comfy beds. It's not uncommon for domesticated dogs to live to fifteen or older. And with old age comes weakening discs, joints and other conditions. This isn't helped by how we breed dogs to give them different sizes and shapes and looks. Certain breeds are more prone to certain problems. For example, we see very young dachshunds with dried-out discs that have exploded their nucleus upwards, which squashes and injures the spinal cord. (The nucleus is like the jam in a dried-out doughnut.) We also see French Bulldogs with spinal deformities.

One breed that is prone to spinal problems is the Dobermann. These loyal, strong, intelligent dogs are often used as guard dogs because they can look quite scary. But as family dogs, they're gentle giants. Roger the Dobermann came to me when he was seven years old. It should have been the prime of his life, but his human guardians had noticed him collapsing on his hind legs. **It was a case of 'Wobbler Disease'**, an apt name because animals with this disease get progressively less steady on their feet and wobble. This is caused by the squashing of the spinal cord in the neck region. Two of the discs in Roger's spine were drying out for genetic reasons and bulging, compressing his spinal cord inside the spinal canal. This was impairing the brain signals going down his spinal cord and reaching his hind legs. The bulging discs were also causing him pain by pinching the nerves that come off the spinal cord at each level to supply various areas, like the front legs, for example. The technical name for this condition is called 'Disc-Associated Wobbler Syndrome', or DAWS for short.

There are a few options when dealing with a condition like this that all come with their own risks and challenges. For example, we can try to cut out a single disc bulge or put in a rigid spacer to replace the disc and fuse the vertebrae together. But, importantly, Roger had *two* dried out bulging discs next to each other. This meant that cutting out two disc bulges would be difficult and fusing the vertebrae in his case could cause problems in other nearby discs. So the family opted for two full

disc replacements.

What evolution had created naturally, I had been seeking to replicate in the design of a new artificial disc for some years. The final model which I used for Roger was inspired by both nature and Captain America's shield.

In an effort to allow movement side-to-side and front-to-back, the 'Fitz-Disc' has two parts:

1. A dome made of a highly polished metal called 'cobalt chromium', backed with a titanium metal mesh that is like a honeycomb which bone grows into. This is screwed to one vertebra and looks a lot like Captain America's shield.

2. A shallow dish made of high-density plastic which also has bone on-growth mesh is screwed to the next vertebra nearby. The curve of this dish matches that of the dome exactly.

The two parts – dome and dish - slide a little

against one another, allowing flexibility. Obviously, I couldn't find vibranium anywhere (that's just a metal of fictional superheroes), but these discs shouldn't wear out and hopefully Roger has many years of pain-free happy running ahead of him.

Ivor and Spiderman's Web

Ivor was the most adorable eight-year-old Maine Coon cat who was hit by a car and had to have one of his hind legs amputated. As we know, most dogs or cats will get along just fine on three legs. But sadly for Ivor, his other ankle, which we now know is the joint between the tibia and the talus and calcaneus bones, was also severely damaged by the accident.

Ivor's ankle collapsed because the talus bone had been destroyed and bacteria then caused an infection within the joint that was eating away more bone. In a cat, like I described for Oscar, the ankle and the arch part of the foot is lifted off the ground to allow cats to jump high – and they stand on their tippy-toes. But with the collapse and only having one hind leg, poor Ivor was dragging himself

around in more and more pain.

By the time I met him, there were three problems to deal with – collapse of the joint, bone loss and infection. First, I operated to remove the infected material from the ankle joint and I packed the hole with dissolvable beads containing antibiotics. Then the lower leg and the foot were supported using wires through the small bones connected to an ESF frame, as for Winston.

Now comes the really cool bit. Once the infection was under control, I took some fat from Ivor's belly and in the laboratory we separated out the pericytes (the small cells that surround blood vessels in fat) from the fat tissue. From these cells we grew very special stem cells in a special culture medium, which is a liquid that provides all the nutrients for cells to grow. These cells became 'osteogenic' stem cells – which can actually *make bone* inside the body!

Fortunately, I thought of my childhood hero Spider-Man. He could wrap anything up with his

1. We made a web-inspired titanium mesh which was exactly the right shape to fill the hole in Ivor's ankle.
2. The stem cells were then attached into the titanium mesh like Spiderman's sticky web.

3. The mesh was held in place by a custom-made plate bent at exactly the angle Ivor would have normally stood.
4. Then Ivor's body did the rest – allowing the cells to grow into bone over the mesh, fusing the joint together.

webs. So, my team and I got creative:

Ivor could then hop around and create plenty of mischief on three legs, thanks to his superhero mesh stem cell solution.

I still love reading comic books and continue to be inspired by them to help the superpets that visit me. I encourage you to be inspired by any of your passions too – books, films, TV shows, comic books, sport . . . whatever it might be – and think about how you can transfer the things you know about your beloved hobby to doing something good for others.

CHAPTER 7
Sometimes Simple is Best

Comic books have given me much inspiration for my work, but there are more everyday sparks of creativity too. **Sometimes the simple solutions are best — and they might be staring you straight in the face!** In this chapter, I'll show you how the world around you is full of ideas . . . if only you open your eyes to its wonders.

With our state-of-the-art diagnostic scans, we can normally see exactly what's going wrong inside an animal patient. I use animations and computer simulations to show the animal's human companion exactly what's wrong. Then I show them what I'm planning during surgery on a screen in my consulting room. I can prepare my surgical team in the same way.

The advances in implant and prosthetic technology mean I can have made-to-measure plates, screws, spacers or joint replacements 3D-printed and delivered to the surgery within days to weeks depending on their difficulty. Quite often we are developing new body parts to either insert or attach to solve difficult challenges.

But sometimes a high-tech solution isn't required. Surgery might involve precision and a steady hand, especially on small animals, but in other ways it's quite brutal. Cutting tendons, draining blood and drilling into bone. **I sometimes feel like a mechanic as much as a surgeon**, going 'under the bonnet' of an animal to fix the problem.

Growing up on the farm in Ballyfin, I watched my daddy improvise with any materials at hand. Calling out the vet was expensive, so he would tackle most problems himself using tried and tested methods passed down through generations.

Daddy was a hoarder – meaning he threw nothing away. For years I recall a piece of twine he used to hold up his trousers like a belt and when it eventually snapped, he used that same piece of twine wrapped around a post to hold a gate shut. Like him, I struggle to dispose of things because, in my head, every little thing might have a use in the future. **You can barely see the floor of my office, for all the odds and ends strewn about.** I have a cupboard I call 'Narnia', after the world inside the fictional wardrobe in C.S. Lewis's book *The Lion, The Witch and the Wardrobe*. We call it that because it seems never-ending. If I can't find a spot for something on the shelves in my office or on a corner of my desk, into 'Narnia' it goes. If I'm in a surgery and we realise we're missing some piece of equipment that might be useful, it can normally be found in that cupboard.

A Splint for Shep

When I was a young farm vet in Ireland, I often had to 'make do'. I once visited an old farmer called Larry to treat one of his cows for mastitis. This is a painful swelling and infection of the udder, which is a bag-like sac under the belly of a cow. This sac produces milk which comes out through the teats, just like the sheep in chapter 1. While I was there, Larry happened to mention his sheepdog had a problem too. He'd been kicked by a grumpy cow and was limping around in obvious pain. I took a look and quickly decided the poor Collie had broken his thigh bone (the femur). I tried to explain I didn't have any of the right equipment on me to help, but Larry insisted I try something.

I took inspiration from a procedure used for soldiers who'd broken their legs in the

First World War, called an 'extension splint'. This involves using looped wires in the groin area and vertical metal struts to extend the leg, so that the broken bone is held in place while it heals together again. I carried out the procedure right there on Larry's kitchen table, using thick, strong wire that he provided and bandages from the boot of my car.

Years later, after having ankle surgery myself, I **tried to create a similar sort of splint for my own leg**, so I could continue standing in order to operate on animals in my care, instead of resting as my doctor instructed (like I said before, I'm *not* a good patient!). I used a child's toilet seat for my buttock, some wire from 'Narnia' to stretch my leg and an old running shoe at the bottom for my foot. I might have looked a bit silly, but my motto is, **'Simple is best. . . if it works.'** Many of my patients look a bit silly too, with half their fur shaved off for an operation, or a brightly coloured bandage or bootie. They don't complain.

They just get on with life, so I do the same.

But that's enough about me and my toilet seat. Let's go and meet some more superpets.

All Buttoned Up

I never throw buttons away. There's a tray of them in Narnia. Simple is best!

Once I was stitching up a cow back in Ireland. I needed to sew two flaps of skin together, so I asked if there were any spare buttons to hold the thread in place without ripping the skin, as I had done with the rubber tubing in Winston. The farmer's wife, with barely a word, cut some lovely big black buttons from her husband's best Sunday coat, and I used them to sew up the cow. She wore them for a few days, before I took the stitches out. Next day they were sewn back on to the man's coat. And why not, I say – they were good buttons!

Like Ivor the cat, my feline companion, Ricochet,

is a Maine Coon – large, with thick, long fur and a bushy tail like a squirrel. Ricochet looks like a small lion, with a dark black-brown mane, huge paws and a sometimes fearsome stare. Unfortunately, he has chronic ear issues, meaning that he will live with them his whole life. When he arrived at five months old, he had a clump of cells called a polyp growing inside the base of his skull, with long tentacles, bursting through his ear drum and ending up in his ear canal. Despite removing the abnormal tissue, he's still prone to inflammation and infection in the area. One time, when it got itchy and sore, he did what we humans would do too – he scratched the itch! Sadly, he scratched his ear flap so much that he

burst the tiny blood vessels inside it, which then bled and created a blood blister in his ear flap, a bit like pumping water into a balloon.

Immediately I thought of buttons.

I cut into the blister to release the build-up of blood and then used buttons from an old shirt in my office and from a teddy bear, sewn on either side, to spread the pressure from stitches and press the skin back on to the cartilage of the ear flap. Five pairs of buttons, like five sandwiches. Ricochet looked quite funny for a while, his ear flap weighed down by an assortment of different coloured buttons. He wasn't very impressed at all. But the procedure was a success, and the skin and cartilage healed together just fine. Now his slightly crinkled ear flap matches his slightly squinty eye – he's my boy, I don't mind what he looks like! – and when he jumps up on my knee and throws his big panda paws around my neck to 'smooch' his nose on mine, there's no better feeling in the world.

A Honey-Coated Horse

Early in my career, I met a horse called Frederick. He was a very gentle soul and competed as an eventing horse (taking on jumps). His rider proudly displayed the many rosettes from their competition victories. Frederick was courageous, trusting his rider and taking on high fences, water jumps and ditches without fear. Unfortunately for Frederick, after one jump he bashed his leg badly against a fence rail and ripped open the skin, exposing the bone beneath.

By the time I saw him, he was in a lot of pain and was leaning against his rider who was distraught at the blood pouring from his wound. She held Frederick as I gave him a sedative injection to calm him and then applied local anaesthetic to the wound so he wouldn't feel any pain. There was no way to stitch the torn skin which was ripped from the bone. A big patch of it had lost its blood supply. I had two major concerns – to stop infection and to promote healing. Remembering an old trick from my youth on the farm, I asked if anyone had any honey to hand. Not to eat, in case you were wondering!

What you might not know is that honey has healing properties. That's why humans have used it for thousands of years, besides for its sweet taste. It provides nutrients to help the body's immune response (the way a body heals itself). Some honeys, like Manuka honey, even kill bacteria. My father used to use it when lambs had skin wounds from catching themselves on barbed wire. Luckily, someone who lived nearby went to fetch some honey from her house. But it was a bit runny and kept pouring off the wound rather than staying in place.

My eyes fell on the cab of a nearby horse lorry. Specifically on a small toy bear perched on the dashboard. It was Paddington, in his blue duffel coat and red hat. You remember what Paddington likes to eat? That's right — marmalade sandwiches! I asked the same lady if she also had some marmalade and a clean bedsheet, and back she went to fetch them. I smeared the sticky marmalade on top of the runny honey, then wrapped the bedsheet over to hold it all together over the wound. **Frederick was being very patient.** The thick marmalade didn't soak through the clean sheet bandage, yet kept the honey in place – and the entire dressing was held by tying the strings and toggles of Paddington's coat above and below Fredericks's knee (the equivalent of a human's wrist).

When I saw Frederick again a couple of weeks later, he was **on the mend and infection free.** The honey and the horse's own immune system were working in tandem. Which just goes to show you don't need modern technology in every situation. Sometimes 'biologic' is even better than 'bionic'.

Marmalade saved the day!

Simple Is Always Best – If it Works.

Sometimes wisdom passed from humans down the ages, like the amazing power of honey, can come to the rescue and is backed up by science. And sometimes ideas spring to my mind from ordinary objects around me or memories from my past. If you are observant of the world around you, and ready to be inspired, creative solutions are everywhere. Often the natural world itself has the answer, if we *choose* to see – and which you *will* see with my next case, Charles the Great Dane. Whatever the inspiration, you should never be ashamed, or feel silly, if some small thing grabs your attention – it might just be the universe trying to tell you something! Sometimes simple inspiration leads to high-tech wizardry.

CHAPTER 8
How Observation Leads to Innovation

Sometimes ideas for implants and prostheses come from the weirdest of places. Often this innovation comes from frustration. I'm often presented with problems for which a solution doesn't exist. And so I invent one. I have failed many times as a surgeon, and when I do fail, I try to think of a better solution. As I've said before, **all successes stand on the shoulders of failure.**

Charles and the Christmas Tree
Charles was a Great Dane. Though only two years old, he was already a giant, with a silver coat, long

spindly legs and droopy ears. He had a big personality to match his stature. Like Roger the Dobermann, Charles was affected by Wobbler Disease, but of a different sort. His problems were caused not by bulging discs pressing on his spine, but because his vertebrae had grown abnormally since birth. Unlike Roger, Charles' disease was called 'Osseous Associated Wobbler Syndrome' (OAWS for short). But, like Roger, this was genetic (meaning it was likely passed down from his parents) which led to bone or 'osseous' deformity as he grew. The malformed vertebrae were squashing his spinal cord at six separate points in his neck and disturbing the nerve signals between his brain and his legs. It was so sad to see the videos his family took of him trying to run, tumbling and face-planting in the grass.

One way to deal with this is to cut away the oddly shaped bone to relieve the pressure, but I had failed with this surgery in the past, especially when a dog was affected by compression at many locations, like Charles.

I turned instead to a different solution – the humble Christmas tree.

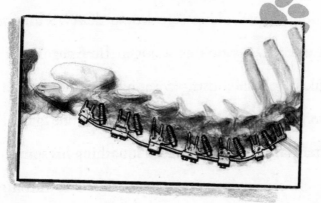

Well, not exactly. I used implants called 'Fitz Intervertebral Traction Screws' (FITS). These are solid thick titanium screws that are driven in *between* the vertebrae like wedges to push them apart – and they look like Christmas trees! By spacing the vertebrae apart, the spinal cord is squashed less by the deformed bone. By then fusing the vertebrae together and removing movement, there is no bending of the squashed spinal cord at the 'pinch-points'. Imagine bending a piece of wire hundreds of times until it snaps – well, that's what effectively happens with the squashed spinal cord at these points without treatment. The 'Christmas tree' spacer screws are secured in place using custom-made saddle-shaped plates screwed to the vertebrae and inspired by a saddle of a horse. Then the plates are linked together using a series of dumb-bells and screw clamps inspired by a trip to the gym. Pay attention to the world, and it will reward you . . .

Still, as with any operation, there are risks. Drilling so close to important nerves and blood vessels is precision work.

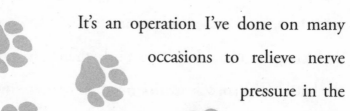

It's an operation I've done on many occasions to relieve nerve pressure in the

spine and the
implant   system
has   improved   over
time, which was just as well,
because Charlie's head was a huge
weight on his neck and I was about to fuse
together almost every vertebra in his neck, so they
would effectively all become one. We anaesthetised
Charles on a very big operating table. We needed
six pairs of Christmas tree spacers, two side-by-side
in between seven of his vertebrae. Operations like
these can seem quite brutal and bloody if you're not
used to them – the drill is noisy and it takes a lot of
force to tighten screws in bone.

Fixing the metal implants in place is only half
the battle. The success of an operation depends on
how well the bone and surrounding tissue heals, and
on keeping the area free of infection. All of Charles'

implants were made from titanium, but no metal, no matter how strong, will hold up if the bone doesn't heal. So it's critical to pack bone marrow around the 'Christmas tree' spacers to fuse all the vertebrae together, as I had done for the Winston's wrists and Milly's toes. I harvested this marrow from the top of Charles' humerus (upper arm) bones just under his shoulders, as I had for Milly. As before, the cells can grow bone and also act as scaffolding into which further bone grows. This spongy tissue from inside your bones is truly 'biological gold dust.' In fact to me, it's more valuable than gold!

After we'd sewn Charlie up, it was an anxious wait to see how he would come round from such a big operation. He was remarkable, and **within a couple of days he was up and walking about** with his very stiff neck. Complete recovery would take a few months, but I was delighted that when his mum and dad brought him to see me for follow-up CT scan, Charlie had gone from a sad and stumbling dog in pain to **a bouncy, happy member of the family** carrying big sticks around in his mouth. The wonderful thing is that dogs have no sense of time. Unlike we humans, they don't worry about the future. They live in the moment. And Charlie was living his new life to the fullest, one happy step at a time. He still is, at the time of writing this book.

The Lollipop and the Engagement Ring

Cancer is a terrible thing, but sadly is very common in dogs and can take many forms. In essence, it's where the growth of a particular type of cell doesn't switch off, and a tumour can form, which is a mass of cells either from that same body part or spreading from another area of the body, which grow into a kind of clump. If it's known as **'benign'** then it can just stay in that area or be cut out, but if it's what is known as **'malignant'**, it can attack the whole body. In my area of expertise, I see bone cancer frequently and it's usually malignant.

When I first met gorgeous big curly-haired Black Russian Terrier Dimitri he was eight years old. His human mum was very fond of him, not least because her husband had sadly died of cancer and Dimitri had kept her company throughout. Now, Dimitri was unable to walk on his left front leg and we had discovered a really bad bone cancer (called 'osteosarcoma') eating away the radius bone of his forearm just above his **carpus** (wrist).

We could have taken off his front leg, but because he was a very large dog, he would have struggled, as dogs bear about sixty per cent of their body weight on their front legs. His mum asked me if I could save his leg. I could have cut off the bottom half of his forearm and implanted a prosthesis as I had done for Betsy, but a better solution would be to just cut out the tumour and replace it with a metal spacer, fusing the bones of his wrist to it as I had done for Winston. The problem was that, until a few years ago, the only metal spacer that was available didn't attach or bond well to the bone and some of my previous patients had suffered failures, meaning that the implant loosened from the bones and the leg collapsed.

On one such day of failure, when I had to amputate the front leg of a large breed dog, I was driving away from my practice very sad and frustrated, when a **lollipop person stepped out in front of me to stop traffic.** I stared at the lollipop, even more frustrated because I was late, while I waited for the pedestrians to cross the road, then I rushed off to the train station. I made the train with seconds to spare and slumped in a seat. As the train pulled off, a beam of sunlight came through the carriage window and landed on a sparkly diamond ring on the hand of a lady sitting opposite me. I closed my eyes – and the universe inspired me. *Of course,* I thought, *a lollipop and an engagement ring!*

When I got back to the practice, with the help of my engineering colleague Jay, I designed something called a 'modular endoprosthesis'. This is a fancy name for a prosthetic that is made of several titanium pieces that can fit together and can be used for any size dog. Here is how it worked:

1. The tumour was eating away the bottom part of the radius bone, which is the front of the two bones in the forearm of the front leg, just above the carpus (wrist) joint. Once the tumour had been cut out by removing the bottom parts of both the radius and ulna bones of the forearm, I filled the space left behind with a box-shaped piece of titanium. The titanium has a surface coating on to which bone can grow.

2. I attached a rod from inside the top of the titanium box to a plate, which I then screwed to what was left of the radius bone, just below the elbow joint.

3. I drilled the cartilage out of the carpus bones (wrist bones) and attached the bottom part of the titanium box across the wrist to the metacarpal bones (palm bones) using a special two-pronged fork-shaped plate and screws.

4. The rod above the titanium box (in point 2) does three things:

   a. It allows me to twist the foot to the correct angle around the rod.

   b. It allows me to stretch the leg to the correct length along the rod – when the leg is in the correct position, the rod is locked inside the titanium box.

   c. It has a metal ring with a nut like an engagement ring on it which is very important, as you will soon see!

5. I screwed another plate to what was left of the ulna bone (the bone at the back of the forearm below the elbow). Then, I used another piece of

titanium, this time shaped like a lollipop, to link the metal (engagement) ring on the radius rod to the ulna plate. In this way the modular implant system wouldn't loosen.

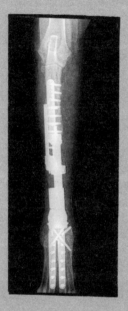 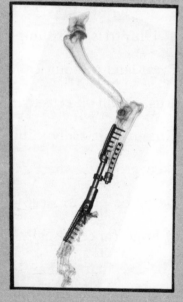

a. I attached the circular bit of the lollipop to the base of the plate on the ulna bone.

b. I attached the stick bit of the lollipop to the engagement ring on the radius rod. The nut on the ring, which looked like the diamond on an engagement ring, locked down on the stick bit, holding the bones tightly together.

By the end of the procedure, the tumour had been removed, and the forearm, wrist and foot were all fused together. All of this from the simple observation of a lollipop and an engagement ring!

Dimitri is still running around happily more than a year later on four legs. He has had chemotherapy drugs to kill off cells that had spread from his initial tumour, but sadly, ultimately other tumours will likely grow elsewhere and, in the end, he will likely die or be put to sleep because of these. His type of bone cancer usually isn't curable. I believe that it may be curable in the future if we can develop better drugs with vets and doctors working together for both animals and humans. For now, Dimitri laps up every single day with his exceedingly long tongue as he runs around happily on four legs.

An Ice Cream Scoop for Bran

From winter to summer, every season brings inspiration. And there's nothing better on a hot summer's day than a big dollop of ice cream. I haven't met a dog yet who wouldn't gobble one up if given half a chance. But for Bran the German Shepherd, it wasn't a real ice cream scoop he needed, but a high-tech one.

Bran was just a puppy, but he'd had a horrible start to life, suffering cruelty from a young age. One of his legs had been broken and left untreated, leading to full-limb amputation (meaning a vet cut off his entire leg). A kind family had adopted him, hoping to give him a happier life going forward, but it was his other hind leg that was now causing him problems. He had developed a condition called 'hip dysplasia'. This happens when the hip socket and the femur (thigh bone) don't fit together properly for genetic reasons. The ball and the edges of the socket of the joint can rub, causing damage to cartilage, pain and significant joint disease. In Bran's case, the joint had dislocated completely, most likely due to his trauma. Now, with only one bad hind leg to stand on, he was in terrible pain, dragging himself along on his front legs.

In situations like this, often vets will suggest putting a dog to sleep, as they did, but Bran's new guardians couldn't bring themselves to do it. **They loved Bran and he was still so young.** Looking into his fluffy face and beautiful eyes, I understood completely. He'd been through so much already and he was ready to fight on.

The only good surgical option for him was a total hip replacement (THR), where the top of the femur is replaced with a metal ball mounted on a stem, and a cup made of dense plastic is provided as a socket for the hip joint. It's an operation that thousands of humans undergo ever year – usually older people whose joints have worn out. In Bran's case, because he only had one hind leg, his foot moved toward the centre of his body, pushing the top part of his femur even further out of the joint. Plus, the muscles around his diseased hip joint were weak as they had never developed properly. So the head of his femur was likely to dislocate from any artificial socket I might use.

But I had already developed a way to prevent this – the 'AceFitz'. The idea had leapt into my brain when I bought ice creams for my work colleagues on a sunny day. The technical name is an 'acetabular augmentation prosthesis', but it looks a bit like an ice cream scoop, with a rounded 'cuplike' shell covered in a special honeycomb titanium mesh. The cup is attached to a long handle, also made of titanium, coated in mineral dust into which bone can permanently grow, becoming part of the body. In a patient with a badly deformed hip socket, like

Bran, I screw the handle of this implant to the side of the pelvis (the 'ilium' – you can feel it below your waist as the hip bone). This was achieved as follows:

1. I drilled out Bran's original diseased cup to expose raw bone like a deep bowl.
2. I placed the metal shell of the 'AceFitz' ice cream scoop implant in this deep bowl and attached its 'handle' plate on to the ilium bone with five screws.
3. Then I sealed a high-density plastic liner in the metal shell at the correct angle using cement.
4. I implanted a titanium mesh-lined stem in the top of the femur bone. This stem had a neck on to which I placed a large, smooth metal head made of cobalt chromium metal.
5. Finally, I put the metal head into the plastic liner. The cup, plus the large shell, provided a ledge so that the head didn't come out of this new hip socket.

Now Bran had a brand new ice cream scoop hip joint! He was out of pain within a week and hasn't looked back since, as he runs around fields and finally got to have a run on the beach and into the sea. He may have seen the worst of human nature, but he's experienced the best too. Through the love of his new family and his own determination to survive, he hopefully has many happy years ahead of him.

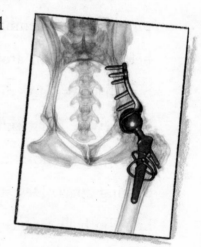

The Terrier and the Tractor Trailer

It's not only everyday objects that inspire me. Sometimes the answers come from memories, like one time on the farm when I almost tipped a trailer of freshly cut barley into a river. That near miss was just the answer I needed for Sunny the Tibetan Terrier!

Tibetan Terriers are an ancient breed that once served as watchdogs outside Buddhist monasteries. Despite his name, Sunny was not a happy dog when I met him. He was in constant pain, after previous knee surgery on his hind legs had failed to fix his problem. The membranes forming the sacs which held the fluid in around his knees were affected by a bad immune disease, which meant that his joints were very inflamed. His knee ligaments were getting more and more damaged and were coming apart. Despite surgery, by the time I saw him, both knees were collapsing. If only one leg had been affected, it might have been possible to remove it. But both of Sunny's hind legs were painful. It was possible to fuse his thigh and shin bones (the femur and tibia) together in one stiff structure, but, unlike Winston who could manage on two fused wrists, Sunny would have had great difficulty with two fused knees. He would not be able to walk properly.

Sunny needed a whole new, moving knee on each side. But, because all of the knee ligaments were diseased, they wouldn't be able to hold together any new knee joint which was just built of metal hinging on plastic. Instead, this hinge between femur and tibia would need to be linked together in some other way.

Luckily, I had a solution, one that I could trace back to my teenage years driving a tractor for my father.

That day, I was sitting high up in the seat of the tractor, pulling a trailer full of freshly harvested barley. I decided I would try to help by driving the trailer out of the field and on to the lane. However, I wasn't as good a tractor driver in reality as I had imagined. At the field exit there was a bridge crossing over a stream. But I took the turn too tightly. The tractor got on to the bridge just fine, but the trailer rode up over the low wall at the edge of the bridge. For a moment, I could hardly breathe, as the trailer wobbled over the water, its axle balanced on the wall, about to spill my precious cargo into the stream. All that stopped it doing so was the tow bar running from the front of the trailer and attached to the back of the tractor.

It was the memory of that heart-in-mouth moment that led to Sunny's solution.

Myself and my colleague Jay invented something called a **'FitzKnee'** – a rotating hinge total knee replacement. As the name suggests, this mechanism took the place of Sunny's knee joint. Here's how it works:

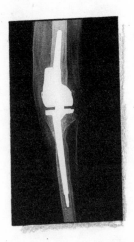
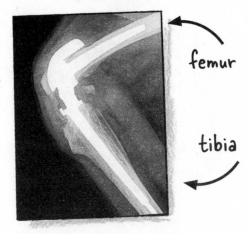

femur

tibia

1. I cut off the ends of both the femur (thigh bone)
   above and the tibia (shin bone) below the knee joint.

2. Then I drilled down into the marrow cavities of
   both bone.

3. I implanted a very smooth curved cobalt
   chromium metal end on to the femur, which in
   turn was attached to a stem that I cemented
   inside the marrow cavity of the bone.

4. I repeated this for the tibia, except that the
   surface here was a flat smooth cobalt chromium
   platform. There was a pillar sticking out of the
   centre of the tibial surface with a hole in it. A

specially shaped high-density plastic spacer was placed over the pillar,

5. Then I placed an axel from the curved femur surface through the hole in the tibial pillar to link these two parts of the implant system together,

6. In this way the two parts of the knee could twist and also hinge against each other.

Because the two metal parts were connected, unlike Sunny's previous knees, the joints could not dislocate, which is pretty amazing!

That day on the farm, my father was furious, but it's nice to think it was all worth it in the end. Thanks to my terrible tractor driving, Sunny had two new knees and once again was living up to his name, smiling every day.

Stevie and Her Skeleton Grabber

When I first met Stevie, a gorgeous six-month-old long-haired dachshund, she couldn't stand on her hind legs and was in significant pain after a horrible accident. She was out walking with her human dad in a park when she was **run over by a bicycle.** Terrified, she ran into traffic and was hit by a car. The collision crushed her pelvis and her sacrum, which is at the very base of the spine. X-ray images followed by CT scans revealed how bad her injuries were. One hind leg was broken, her pelvis was shattered into more than twenty pieces and her sacrum was badly crushed. I was very worried about the nerve supply to her rear end. If this was severed, then there really would be nothing we could do except euthanise, because she'd never be able to walk again or go to the toilet properly. I discussed euthanasia with her family, but they wanted to try their best for her.

First, we undertook the complex procedure of

trying to stabilise the very small fragments of bone in Stevie's sacrum. Using tiny pins held together with a clump of cement, we managed to fix them. And that was just the start. Her pelvis still looked like a jigsaw with its pieces scattered in many directions.

A few days later I performed a second five-hour operation to put the jigsaw together. I have been mending fractures of the pelvis with ESF outside the body, like I used on Milly, Winston and Hero, since the early 1990s. But this particular kind of ESF is very different. As I've said, I love to find inspiration in everyday objects and my original idea for this came from those giant grabbers that we use to pick up metal in scrapyards.

For Stevie, the prongs of the grabber were actually pins that stuck outside the skin in many directions and were attached together using rods and clamps. The whole construct would form a giant 'biological grabber' holding the broken pieces of the pelvis together from outside the body!

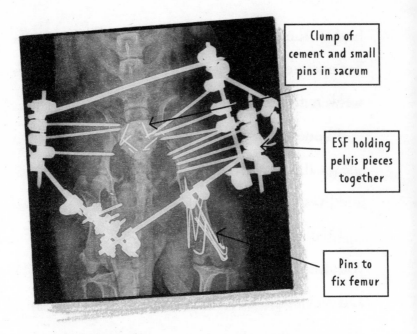

Clump of cement and small pins in sacrum

ESF holding pelvis pieces together

Pins to fix femur

I painstakingly skewered each small piece with some pins and, bit by bit, I realigned the jigsaw of the pelvis by attaching the pins in a frame using rods and clamps on top of the pelvis.

There were so many times we all doubted Stevie could pull through, or worried she would never walk again, but she surprised us all with her bravery and determination. She conquered infection from bugs she'd picked up on the road at the time of her accident but, unfortunately, while the bones healed, the nerve damage she suffered meant that her operated hind leg still didn't work. In the end, we were forced to amputate the limb.

I honestly don't think that Stevie cares at all that she's a three-legged dog. She's grateful for her life and lives each day full of extraordinary bouncy joy.

Once again, just observing the world around you can inspire great innovation, like the grabber and Stevie's pelvic ESF.

CHAPTER 9
Weird and Wonderful

These days, it's mainly cats and dogs who come through the doors of Fitzpatrick Referrals, but over the course of my career I've studied or treated all sorts of animals. I'm lucky that my work has taken me all over the world. I will do my best to treat any animal that comes to me in need, provided it falls within my areas of expertise. And for me, these areas have changed over the years from general to specialist expertise.

One such animal was an African grey parrot, who was brought to me when I was a young general practice vet. The poor bird was suffering from a lung infection and needed to have X-ray images taken.

Normally we'd give an animal a sedative to keep him or her still, but this bird had trouble breathing and anaesthetic was considered too risky. So I had to hold the parrot down under the X-ray machine, wearing gloves lined with lead and a gown to protect my hands and body from radiation. He kept trying to bite me and shout rude words at me, so I accidentally told him to shut his beak. Afterwards, as I handed him back to the lady who'd brought him in, he jumped up on her arm and promptly told her to

'shut your beak'!

I was very embarrassed.

Spiky Friends

I've also worked with animals sent in from local animal sanctuaries, such as foxes and badgers.

Hedgehogs are my personal favourite. I rescued my first when I was a boy living on the farm, taking the hedgehog from the side of the road and feeding him in the barn until one day he wandered off. There's something about these shy and rarely seen creatures that I find fascinating.

In Gaelic, the native language of Ireland, a hedgehog is called a 'grainneog', which means 'ugly one'. I never understood that – I think they're the cutest animals! But as we've built more houses and roads, and with more cars clogging those roads than ever, the little hedgehogs are struggling. Added to the destruction of their natural habitats in hedgerows (from where they get their name), the chemicals we use on our crops cause problems for their food supply too. Hedgehogs eat insects, but **pesticides** (the word means 'pest-killers') kill the insects, meaning the hedgehogs can't find enough to eat.

In the 1950s, there were an estimated 30 million hedgehogs in the UK. Now it's less than a million and numbers are dropping still. In my youth, they were a common sight, but **I doubt many children today have ever seen one in the wild**, other than squashed on a country road. **Have you?**

If we don't do something to reverse the decline, hedgehogs will be extinct in less than fifty years' time. That would be a terrible shame.

The first hedgehog I ever treated as a vet came to my attention as I drove to a lecture one evening. He was struggling at the side of a road, and I quickly realised why – his hind leg was broken, very likely following a run-in with a car. Of course, left in the wild, he would have died a slow and painful death from infection or starvation, or at the teeth of a fox. A hedgehog can't run from a predator, so relies on curling into a tight ball, coated in spines that say, 'You really don't want to eat *this*, do you?' A broken leg would stick out, perfect to be grabbed.

That evening I missed my lecture, taking the injured hedgehog back to my practice. I pinned the bone in place using a special kind of ESF (see page 109), which I made up. It looks like a large safety pin. The long needle bit goes down into the tibia bone

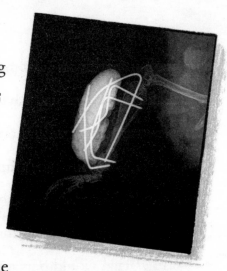

to align it, is bent over at the knee and then attached to smaller pins placed at right angles on the outside of the bone using plumbers' putty, which hardens rapidly. It's very tricky, because a hedgehog's tibia is only a few millimetres wide (that's TINY!). It took a few weeks before we could remove the frame, but we sent a happy hedgehog on his way again.

I've performed the procedure on many hedgehogs since – including those that have broken both back legs! There's no better feeling than watching the little spiky animals shuffle into the undergrowth once more, vanishing out of sight, as if we've just temporarily interrupted their day.

Hedgehogs sometimes need our help, especially over the autumn and winter, when they hibernate. If you see one out and about between December and March, his or her nesting site might have been disturbed. If they're somewhere dangerous, like near a road, or if they look poorly or injured, you can make a temporary hedgehog home to keep them safe.

Use a high-sided cardboard box lined with something soft like a towel or scrunched-up newspaper. Put the hedgehog gently inside (you might have to wear thick gloves so you don't get spiked!) and keep it somewhere warm. Avoid handling the hedgehog too much, because he or she will be scared. A hedgehog can eat meaty dog or cat food, but only offer them water to drink in a dish.

Then contact a hedgehog charity or call a local wildlife sanctuary. They will tell you what to do next.

The Dragon's Wobble

Another strange arrival, in my early days, was a beautiful chameleon dragon. It's so long ago, I can't recall his name. But let's call him 'Frank' for this story. Chameleon dragons are neither chameleons nor dragons (obviously!); they can't breathe fire, but they *can* change colour to blend in with their environment. That was the last thing on Frank's mind when his human companions brought him to see me. Frank had a tumour on his chin. This is usually simple to remove, but there was a complication. The tumour was interfering with the flap of skin under his throat called a 'dewlap'. Male chameleon dragons use this flap to attract a female. By wobbling their dewlap, puffing up their throats, and doing head bobs and push-ups, they are telling females, 'Hey, check me out!'

I don't think Frank knew about his tumour at

all – despite his almost 360-degree vision, he couldn't see under his own chin. But I fancy what he did know was that **his dewlap wobble wasn't quite what it once was.** So I had to be very careful to not only remove the tumour before it grew bigger, but also to stitch up the dewlap in such a way that his love song – or rather his love 'wobble' – wasn't affected. I doubt Frank ever met a female chameleon dragon – they're not common pets! – but if he did, I hope she was impressed.

Hermes, the Abandoned Tortoise

I've inserted implants and attached prostheses on hundreds of cats and dogs, but **Hermes the tortoise was one of my toughest challenges.** When I first met him, he was in a terrible state. Tortoises hibernate each winter; they normally emerge, hungry and excited to get going (as fast as a tortoise can) in spring. But poor Hermes had undergone a grisly, horrible time – rats had found and attacked him during his long sleep and chewed off all but one of his feet. His mum had taken him to a vet who specialised in exotic animals, but all she'd been able to do was clean the wounds and give him medication to prevent infection. With only one foot, Hermes couldn't walk and didn't have a quality of life. His vet knew I specialised in prosthetic limbs, so I was Hermes' last hope.

I'd worked on tortoises before and learned lots about their care. There were some options, but none of them were suitable. One was wheels, but that needed two working feet so Hermes could propel himself. Another idea was to use prosthetic legs which simply slotted over the existing stumps – stump socket prostheses. On another animal this may have worked, but Hermes needed to be able to retract his flexible limbs into his shell. The prosthetics would simply fall off.

The answer was prosthetics that actually attached to the remaining bones of the legs permanently. This was a challenging operation, which I don't think had ever been attempted on a tortoise before. His mum and I talked about it long and hard, going over the risks of surgery on multiple occasions. **She had found him abandoned in a cardboard box from the delivery company Hermes.** She wanted him to have a chance, but, as for all cases, we only ever operate in the animal's best interests. There were risks that Hermes' bones might be too delicate to support the metal rods of the implants, or his skin might not grow well on to the implants, or infection may come back. His own vet, his mum, another exotic animal specialist and myself all considered deeply whether the kindest option *might* be to put him to sleep.

Hermes was only five years old — young for a tortoise of his type — and if he pulled through the surgery, he might have another forty years of happy life ahead. In the end, after lots of thought, we made an appropriate plan for Hermes and proceeded with surgery. I assembled a team including my exotics specialist colleague, who scrubbed into the operation with me, an anaesthetist, various nurses and intern vets, and together we performed the procedure. It went well, and afterwards Hermes was moved to his very own specially heated and lighted ward for recovery. **Within a week he was moving around** using the metal spigots which stuck out through the skin from the implants inside, before we even attached new rubber feet on the outside.

Hermes is a good example of what I spoke about earlier on ethics and how many vets have different opinions on what is right. When some vets saw Hermes' operation on my TV show, they brought a legal challenge against me accusing me of not looking after his welfare properly, because they believed passionately that the best thing for Hermes was to put him to sleep. My colleagues, Hermes' mum and myself believed passionately that we should try to help him. As I try to move medicine forward for the benefit of animals, some vets may feel I am guilty of 'over-treatment' or being 'unethical' – perhaps even with some of the patients I describe in this book, like Hermes. You will need to decide for yourself what you think is the 'right thing to do' for animals going forward.

I still feel confident that collectively we did the right thing for Hermes. Unfortunately, some months after the operation, he became ill and sadly died. This time it was an internal problem that was unrelated to the operation. **We'd hoped that we could give Hermes a long life,** but in the end all he got were a few months with his new legs. Everyone involved was really upset – we'd been through so much together, and we had done our best for Hermes.

The Broken Buzzard

Buzzards are the UK's most widespread bird of prey. These magnificent creatures can be seen soaring over the countryside in search of their dinner – normally rodents, rabbits or smaller birds. So when a wildlife charity brought an injured buzzard to us, even though I'm not a bird specialist, I wanted to help. **The poor bird had collided with a power line** and scans revealed it had a fracture in

one of its wing bones. Needless to say, a buzzard who can no longer fly would die very quickly in the wild, because it could not hunt.

Did you know, some bird bones are actually hollow? The technical word is pneumatised. Instead of being dense and solid like our bones, there are pockets of air inside, criss-crossed by struts of bone like scaffolding. This makes the bones extra strong, able to withstand the pressures of flight, but the bones also work with the lungs to get oxygen all around the body, providing extra energy for flight.

It never ceases to amaze me how much all animals, including us humans, have in common. A buzzard has a humerus (upper arm bone) as well as a radius and ulna in the forearm like you and me, but these have evolved into a wing rather than an arm. The buzzard had broken his humerus bone near to his chest, in an area that was difficult to reach. Added to that, surgery would have to be very precise, because a bird's bones are brittle and the main blood supply to the buzzard's wing ran over the site of the fracture. If I accidentally damaged this, any operation to repair the wing would be pointless.

We anaesthetised the buzzard and then plucked the feathers around the injury. It took a while to place a pin in his bone to realign the broken bits, and it was still an anxious wait to see how he would be when he woke up from anaesthesia. Unlike with a human patient, you can't tell a bird to rest and relax, so **we bandaged the wing to his body to stop him from flapping it**, which would twist his bone and prevent it from healing properly.

After a short stay at the practice, the wildlife charity took him away to continue his recovery. Now it was up to mother nature and time to help him heal. I'm so happy to tell you that six weeks later, X-ray images revealed the bone fracture had healed, and the last of the bandages were off. Seeing the graceful and beautiful bird take to the sky once more made my heart soar as well.

Guardians of the Planet

As I have mentioned, one of my central beliefs is that we can translate our love for our animal companions in our homes into love for wild animals in their homes too. Being able to care deeply about others, for no personal gain, is what makes us most *human*. No gain, means 'unconditional' – and that's why it's called unconditional love. Our companion animals share this with us every day and I feel it's only right to give it back. It's my dream to somehow extend this love into caring for the planet as a whole – building a *community of compassion* for animals – and for people we might never meet. We are all connected, after all – as inhabitants of planet earth. This is true in the scientific sense, because we all inhabit an ecosystem, where one person's actions have knock-on effects on others. But I think it's true on a much deeper level too.

When families are in my practice with a poorly animal companion, they forget all about their other problems – their squabbles and worries – because the cat or dog they love is in pain. **Everyone is joined together in fear regarding the possible outcome for the animal they love so deeply, and in so uniting they are also joined together in hope and in love – which is a magnificent thing.** When I care for an animal, when I take away their pain, I see such joy and love in their human families. Imagine if we could spread that love around the world. Imagine if we all tap into that *oneness,* where everyone is joined and guided by love. I call it the *universal string of oneness* that connects every living thing.

I was lucky enough recently to make a trip to Africa, where I saw wild animals in their natural habitats. You probably know that many of the creatures of the savanna are endangered because of humans. Climate change, the shrinking of their habitats and poaching all mean that it's harder and harder for wildlife to thrive. But many people are fighting back. Huge tracts of land have been set up to protect creatures at risk from poaching, animals are tracked with remote radio sensors to make sure they're safe and population numbers are closely monitored. This couldn't happen without many dedicated humans all working together, **working as one**. And to see the hope and passion in their eyes was utterly inspiring. As well as volunteers and rangers, veterinary professionals can treat disease and injuries before releasing animals back into the wild or caring for them in a sanctuary. We have messed around with nature and the habitats of animals so much, we absolutely should step in and step up to fix the problems of our own making as best we can.

If your family does get the chance to go see some of these animals in Africa, please remember to only pay for a holiday where the money goes to the local communities, so that they can afford to look after the animals better. That's sustainable tourism.

Rici the Big-Hearted Lion

On my trip I met an animal who'll stay with me forever. Rici the lion had been rescued from captivity, where neglect and poor nutrition had caused him painful joint problems. It seemed only right that this beautiful creature, who'd been taken from the wild and experienced the worst of human nature, should be given a chance to live his remaining years with proper care, with the grass of the plains beneath his paws. So, I found myself – the boy who had made up stories about Vetman and his adventures with a big-hearted lion – standing over the anaesthetised body of a real one.

Nothing could have prepared me for the sheer size of Rici, with his **magnificent mane and paws way bigger than dinner plates**. To treat his condition, we gave him injections into his worn joints, a combination of:

- 🐾 **Platelets**, which are tiny disc-shaped pieces of bone marrow cells in the bloodstream that had been extracted from his own blood.

- 🐾 A man-made viscoelastic lubricant, which is a material that helps worn joint surfaces to slide past one another without rubbing so much.

I wished we'd had access to the types of anti-inflammatory stem cells that I could grow from fat tissue in the laboratory at my own practice, but sadly that wasn't yet available for lions in Africa. Still, we did our best to make him happier.

When I got home, another Rici was less than happy though. My cat Ricochet's eyes narrowed when he sniffed me. He knew I'd been spending time with a cat who wasn't him! Even worse, this other Rici had a bigger mane and bigger paws than Ricochet (who I also call Rici for short). Maybe Ricochet doesn't understand the *universal string of oneness* that holds us all together, or maybe he just wants his dad around all the time. I didn't blame him, and I knew he'd forgive me . . . which he did sooner rather than later.

Dogs and cats are by far the most popular pets in the UK. There are over 10 million of each, most of them beloved members of their families. I hope in my lifetime, by example and by writing books like this, to show people that all animals deserve our love, care and respect on this beautiful and fragile planet.

I've been privileged to encounter so many different species over the years, who all meant something special to their human guardians or are very special parts of natural ecosystems. They've all taught me something too – they've been the greatest teachers about *love*. **Finding a solution to their injuries and illnesses and taking away their pain is why I became a vet in the first place.** As I've said before, if you spend your life doing something that you love, you need never work a day in your life. There's no better feeling than seeing an animal on the path to a better life.

That's not to say, however, that there aren't some moments I'd rather forget. You'll see in the next chapter what I mean.

CHAPTER 10
Supervet Perils

There are some benefits to being on TV, but the day-to-day work as a vet is far from glamorous! Surgery is a messy, blood-spattered business, when you're working inside an animal or dealing with horrible injuries. And you can be sure the gore will sometimes find its way past all the gowns and gloves and masks we wear.

When I'm operating, someone is constantly on standby with swabs to soak up blood and a suction tube to suck it away from the area of the operation. But sometimes there are surprises. Scar tissue (just like the scars you can get after a bad fall) can hide blood vessels inside them. The pathways of the blood vessels may be changed by the scar tissue or you just can't easily see them, and if they get nicked by a scalpel blade, the blood can squirt all over the place – in your eyes, even on the ceiling!

Blood is hardly the worst part though. Animals that are poorly do not care about what they cover you with! I get weed on most weeks and poo, snot, drool and vomit are all regular parts of my day. I hardly notice for the most part – growing up on a farm prepares you for anything. My mother sometimes wouldn't let us in the house until we'd stripped off to our underwear outside because we were covered in smelly muck.

From Head to Toe

By far the most disgusting moment of my career working with large animals came at the back end of an angry cow. One of my jobs was inspecting and treating cows' hooves. Hooves can become overgrown or ingrown, but the most common problem is infection in the hoof itself. This happens for all sorts of reasons, but often because of the moist and muddy environments in which cows spend much of their lives. The wall of the hoof can get soft and crack, or the cow might stand on a sharp stone or nail that penetrates the horn (the wall of the hoof). Once bacteria get into the wound, they can cause a painful build-up of pus (yellow or green gooey liquid) called an 'abscess'. Cows are such heavy animals that a problem with the hoof can have other effects, putting pressure on joints higher up the leg and making the cow lame (having difficulty walking).

The solution is to cut away the dead or damaged horn before treating and cleaning the site of infection. It's important not to cut too deep, as you risk cutting into the 'corium', which is the sensitive

part that creates new hoof and is filled with blood vessels. Sometimes special blocks are attached to the hoof as well with glue, to build it back up and let the cow walk properly – a 'cow shoe'.

I treated many hundreds of cows in the early part of my career in farm animal practice. On this particular occasion, I had been working hard all day, delivering calves and lambs, and didn't have time until after dark to go to trim the painful hooves of a cow on a farm in Ireland. The cow was held in a chute, which is a sort of cage, whilst I stood behind her, my back to her rump, her back foot on my knee, as I pared and filed off her overgrown hooves bit by bit, illuminated by the lights of a tractor shining on me. All of a sudden, I must have hit a sensitive spot, because she kicked out at me, lifted her tail and pooed diarrhoea. Unfortunately for me, because of my position, that meant that she actually **pooed on my head. I was covered from head to toe** in diarrhoea. Yuck! As I wiped poo from my ears and eyes, I realised that was the end of my large-animal veterinary career. I just wasn't cut out for it.

Gross-Out: Pee, Poo, Vomit, Snot and Spit

There's still plenty of poo to deal with in primary care practice and at Fitzpatrick Referrals, but it tends not to come in quite such large amounts, nor is it directed at my head! I was once due to leave for the day to go and do a TV interview after an operation on a puppy. I changed out of my scrubs and into the only pair of smart, clean trousers I had. But I wanted to check on the recovering puppy one last time, so went to the ward kennels to see him. And he looked at me with such sad little eyes that I couldn't help giving him a cuddle. Of course, that was the moment he chose to relieve himself, all over my clean trousers!

Vomit is an everyday occurrence in a vet's life too. Dogs and cats can throw up if they have upset stomachs, a reaction to certain medicines, if they swallow something that irritates their tummies or if they're anxious, just like humans.

In my years in general practice, a common visitor would be a dog or cat that had swallowed something they shouldn't. Some breeds – like Labradors – are known for eating anything that gets close to their mouth, whether it be dog food, human food or not food at all – like bits of slippers! Chocolate, though, seems a common choice for dogs and sometimes cats who find their way to the vet – it tastes good to animals too! But it can be very dangerous, as it contains a chemical compound called 'theobromine', which is toxic and can be poisonous for dogs and cats in large enough amounts.

I remember one boy and his mum coming in with their dog, who coughed up two socks. 'Told you!' the boy said. Apparently, his mother had always blamed him for having **odd socks,** but now he had proof it wasn't his fault after all.

Sometimes vets have to give a dog or cat an 'emetic', a medicine to *make* them vomit. Once a worried young couple brought their canine companion in to see me. They'd lost an engagement ring worth thousands of pounds; they blamed their furry friend. And he *did* look guilty, or maybe he was confused about why everyone looked so cross with him! The story was that he'd spotted a bun left on a bedside table and taken a fancy to it, gobbling it up before anyone could stop him. Unfortunately, on the same table beside the bun, the woman had left her ring. Sure enough, a few minutes after receiving the emetic, the dog was throwing up both the remains of the bun and a rather lovely piece of jewellery. We gave it a wash and placed it where it belonged, on the woman's finger. I'm sure she's been more careful since, and I hope the diamond thief learned his lesson. Somehow, I doubt it.

But sometimes it's trickier to remove things from inside animals and an emetic just won't do. One method is to use an endoscope (a long flexible tube with a light and camera at the end):

1. First, we give the animal a sedative or anaesthetic.

2. Then we push the endoscope down their **oesophagus** (food pipe) and even into the stomach. This helps us find blockages.

3. We might even insert a grabber inside or alongside the scope to remove small objects once we hit the bottom. I once took out a small breadknife this way by grabbing and then pulling both the scope and the knife backwards!

You'd be surprised at what a dog can swallow! Sometimes surgery can be the only way to remove things from deeper in the dog's digestive tract. In my years of general practice I saw plenty of **tennis balls, plastic containers (that had once contained food), hats and gloves, bits of shoe, pebbles and leaves and toy figures** all removed from the small intestine by open surgery.

If a dog or a cat swallows string, ribbon or tape, it can be very serious because the gut can bunch up like a caterpillar along objects such as these. Once I treated a very curious puppy called Rufus. He was adorable but very naughty, and when his family weren't looking, he tipped over the kitchen bin, rifled through it and ate a long piece of string that had been used to wrap a juicy piece of meat. The string got caught up in his small intestine, which is the long tube where food passes before you poo! This then caused a hole where the digested food and poo from the intestine leaked and caused an infection known as 'peritonitis', which nearly killed him. He was on a drip and had to take antibiotics after the surgery for several days. He was very lucky to make it through. His family locked the kitchen bin in a cupboard after that!

One particular Labrador named Fred sticks in my mind too. His human mum and her son came to see me. The lad was upset because **Fred had devoured an entire Lego castle** that had taken a long time to build. I performed surgery, finding bits of the plastic throughout his small intestine. Fred was soon stitched up and happy and his Mum was relieved. But the boy wasn't so pleased. Though I'd recovered most of the Lego pieces, we were missing some bits of the turret. They must have already come out of his rear end. The embarrassed look in Fred's eyes said it all!

I love all dogs, big and small, but it's fair to say the larger breeds can be harder to handle, and a lot messier. I've been drenched in snot from a sneezing Great Dane, and I'll never forget George the St Bernard. As anyone who lives with this gentle, giant breed will tell you, it's important to have a cloth or towel at hand most of the time. That's because they can drool *a lot*. I was trying to change the bandages on one of George's legs, but he was doing his best to escape. In our tussle, he shook his head from side to side like a toddler having a tantrum. With each swish of his enormous muzzle, great strands of saliva like the tentacles of a writhing octopus were looping from his jaws and wrapping themselves around my head. I certainly needed a towel after that. Thanks, George!

Dogs can get plenty of problems with their ears too, which are more exposed and floppier than ours, plus dogs go places where things can get inside their ear canal. Commonly it's grass seeds, which can cause infections and blockages. This can be easy or hard to treat, depending how deep inside the ear the problem lies. **A pair of forceps is sometimes enough to clear a blockage, or some light suction.**

As a boy on the farm, I used to watch my father using a hosepipe to siphon diesel fuel from one vehicle to a container in order to transfer it to another. This involves inserting the hose into one fuel tank, then sucking on the other end to get the fuel flowing. The trick is to stop sucking at just the right moment so you don't get a mouthful (don't try this at home!). Once, in my very early career, I was in general practice and didn't have an appropriate syringe to hand when I was asked to clear a hairy dog's ears on a remote farm using a similar method.

Unfortunately, I didn't stop sucking soon enough. Yep, that's right – I got a mouthful of liquid wax. In case you were wondering, the taste of infected ear wax is not pleasant!

Teeth, Claws and Dangerous Hooves

I'm no stranger to being bitten by dogs or cats. Animals in pain are often scared or traumatised by whatever has befallen them. **Put yourself in their shoes**, being brought by their human companions to a place they don't recognise, filled with people they've never met wearing strange clothes. We may not be able to smell the other animals, but you can be sure a dog's sensitive nose is picking up all the other creatures in the surrounding rooms, and their super hearing is picking up strange sounds from everywhere around them. The same is true of an irritated cat. I have more than a few cat scratch scars to prove that talking softly to your patient as a vet isn't always effective!

In the early days of my career, I treated quite a few horses as a general practice vet. I enjoyed helping to deliver foals, calming the mare as she brought new life into the world. I wasn't much good at shoeing though (taking off old horseshoes and putting on new ones), and I dreaded rasping horses' teeth. You have to shave off the points and edges of the cheek teeth and the horse normally doesn't like it much either. They're prone to give you a headbutt, and every now and then one might try to chomp off your hand. But **it's the back end of horse that you have to worry about the most**. My career with my equine friends ended badly when trying to load one particularly irritated horse into a horsebox. He was having none of it and kicked me square in the middle of my chest, sending me flying backwards on to the concrete, cracking two of my ribs. I decided ultimately that horse practice wasn't for me either.

Doggy Dating

Dogs are wary observers of the world, with their own set of rules for interacting. For example, dogs rarely stare each other in the eye, unless they're trying to be challenging or intimidating, so it's best not to look deeply into theirs unless you know them really well. **They respond to body language**, and fast or unexpected movements can startle them and make them nervous. Scientists who study animal behaviour have shown that dogs respond to different facial expressions in humans – smiles and frowns, as well as the tone of voice used. This isn't surprising given how long humans and dogs have lived side by side. Dogs have had to learn which humans mean them harm and which are friendly, and I firmly believe they're very good judges of character.

I don't hold a bite or scratch against any animal. It's their way of saying, 'Keep away from me, stranger!' It can be hard to earn a dog's trust, especially when they're shy or afraid. My method is to keep my distance and crouch or kneel at their level without looking directly at them. That makes me look smaller and less intimidating. Then I just wait calmly and let the dog come into my

space, rather than invading theirs. If they're wary or hesitant to come nearer to me, I just give them time to settle down. When they do approach, I respond calmly without any sudden

movements. Also, I'm very careful where I touch them and never do it in a pushy or intrusive way. Most of the time it works.

I call the process 'doggy dating' – getting to know one another.

For humans it's different, and unless you're very familiar with dogs, it can be hard to work out what they're thinking. An angry, shy or scared dog may bark differently to an excited or happy one. Baring teeth can be a threat or a submissive gesture. Yawning rarely means tiredness in a dog, but shows they're anxious. We've all seen a happy dog wagging its tail so hard its bum can't keep up, but to another dog the position or speed of a tail wag has hidden meanings we humans find tricky to understand.

No animal, in my opinion, is born 'bad' – but many have been treated badly or are simply shy or scared. Sometimes with patience we can help them relax, but other times in the short period I get to see them as a vet in my practice, it can be impossible, without more time. However, I believe it's my duty always to try. I have to remember that I'm often seeing a dog or cat at a particularly bad moment in their life. They deserve our respect and our kindness at all times.

Ralph's Rescue Remedy

With Ralph, I had my work cut out. He was an *enormous* Neapolitan Mastiff, with a wrinkled brow, droopy jowls and a face that couldn't have looked less impressed with me. This was probably because I had to keep injecting him. Wouldn't you dislike a man who kept sticking a needle in you? As part of his treatment, we had to keep him in our ward kennels overnight for several days. He was showing what we call 'kennel guarding behaviour'. This is when a dog is aggressive if you approach his or her living space – snapping, growling and lunging at the door. Most dogs, if they're nervous about a person, will move away, but a cage or kennel compartment won't allow that, so they can feel trapped, becoming fearful and anxious. In such cases, all they have left to react with is their voice and body language. Ralph the giant probably weighed almost as much as I do, and with such a massive breed, you have to be careful they don't hurt you or themselves.

When I started Fitzpatrick Referrals, I built kennel wards with bacterial resistant wipe-down compartments and the hardened see-through glass doors I mentioned before, instead of keeping animals in cages with bars. **We have lovely soft blankets and a radio on for the dogs**. The larger compartments even have televisions to make their stay at what I call the 'Fitz-Ritz Hotel' as much like home as possible.

This results in much less anxiety and much less collective barking. But even with all of the normal soothing measures, Ralph wasn't having any of my kind efforts.

I want every canine patient to trust me and I don't like to admit defeat with any dog, but Ralph was a challenge. My tactic was to go and sit right beside his door, ignoring Ralph's drooling angry face as I ate my sandwiches. When he realised I wasn't interested in him, threatening him or challenging in any way, he'd calm down. I'd use this opportunity to slip a little of my sandwich through the gap in his door and mutter a few kind words, but never looking directly at him. At first, this would just set off more barking and lunging, pawing at the door with his monster paws.

But Ralph was in with us for a while, so time was on my side. Nightly, **I'd eat beside him,** ignoring his glaring eyes, sharing my meal. And after a few days, I could even open the door a fraction without him attacking me. I'd like to say this story ends with Ralph enjoying a belly tickle, but we never quite reached that stage. I'd say he 'put up with me'. He wasn't so wary of the strange human who liked to eat sandwiches on the floor any more.

Life as a vet, like life in general, throws up all sorts of surprises. The most important thing is to be ready to try your best, to compromise, to be kind and to always try to do the right thing.

Extraordinary situations can be stressful and uncertain, but they're opportunities to learn and adapt as well. If you find yourself facing something new, take a deep breath, clear your head and put your best paw forward!

The Stranded Swan

I was in Dublin, Ireland, rushing in a taxi to an important interview on a very rainy day, when a swan mistook the rain pooling on the slick surface of a road for the local canal. Unfortunately, that caused the poor fellow to land smack wallop in front of a truck, a motorbike and many cars on a very busy four-lane road. His only saving grace was that the lights were red and the **Supervet was in a taxi.** I jumped out and rushed toward the confused and bewildered bird. I wasn't worried about being hit myself – it never crossed my mind! That's a peril of being me – I just jump right in, especially if an animal is in trouble.

You have to be careful with swans – they don't know when you're trying to help them, so they might **hiss and bite**. Fortunately for me, I had history herding sheep back on our farm in my childhood – they also don't know what's good for them! So I flailed my hands about to stop all the traffic and used my jacket as a blanket to 'herd' the swan off the road and on to a footpath on a smaller side road – just as I used to do with the sheep. Finally, I cornered him in a churchyard. Then, quick as a flash, I threw my jacket over him and bundled his wings together. At the same time I grabbed his neck so he couldn't bite me.

I held him close to my chest, inside my jacket, and carried him as fast as I could back up the road toward the canal. I was proud as punch as I released him back on to the water. Watching him swim away made me feel like a swan superhero as I flapped my jacket open and popped it back on. My elation was short-lived however, as I realised that the swan had pooed all down the inside of my jacket. And it wasn't a small poo – it was a giant splatter of swan stress diarrhoea. It was all over my white shirt, and I couldn't take it off because in twenty minutes I was going to be interviewed live on national radio!

Needless to say, I was squirming (and smelly!) in the interview chair, with a giant streak of swan poo running down by back. Still, this particular 'tragedy' turned out to be amazing because in my interview I was talking about one of my core beliefs: that human and animal medicine should work together because we're all just animals really – 'Humanimals'. I never would have gained any newspaper coverage just for that – but I sure did with the headline 'Supervet to the rescue of stranded swan in Dublin'. So my swan friend taught me to look on the bright side of life – **even when you are pooed on, life might be doing you a favour**! This was a swan song that everybody heard – the message of Humanimality.

Humanimality and One Medicine

In 2014, I founded Humanimal Trust, a charity to promote the idea that vets, doctors and medical researchers could work together to drive forward medical progress. This is a concept called 'One Medicine' as mentioned in chapter 3, where animals benefit equally from all medical advances, from stem cells to bionic legs.

I want to share what I'm learning being a vet at the forefront of surgery for the benefit of human medicine and I **want animals to benefit from the implant and drug technologies that are given to humans** through experiments on animals. Most people don't like to think about the link between animal experimentation and the drugs and implants we give to humans. Nearly every single antibiotic or cancer drug used for treating a human, or any implant to replace a diseased human joint, has been tested on a healthy animal who is given a disease and then sadly killed

– just for human benefit. The first thing I would like to achieve in my lifetime is to try to make the drugs and medical technology we use for humans available for the animals we love too. That seems fair, don't you think, given animals helped us develop them in the first place? For example, replacement of the shoulder joint for arthritis (which as we've learned is a painful disease due to inflammation of a joint) was performed as an experiment on dogs for human benefit more than seventy years ago, but still today, I'm the only surgeon in the world offering shoulder replacement implants to dogs that really need them. I don't think this is fair.

The second thing I would like to achieve is to help the charity I founded to reduce the number of animals bred or used purely for testing procedures and treatments, by encouraging everyone to share their knowledge, especially people who study naturally occurring diseases in animals, which are very similar to those in human beings. Things can't happen overnight – but if we try hard to understand what is actually happening right now and really want to make change, we can improve things for the better.

Sadly, the law says that experimental animals are the *only* way to test many drugs and implants for humans. I would like to help create a legal structure for vets working with animals who already have diseases and need treatment, so that they can have new drugs and implants which could be better than what we have now. This structure could really help sick animals rather than just giving the drugs and implants to healthy animals who do not need them, purely for human benefit. This new system would need to have proper legal paperwork to protect vets and families and would also need to make enough money for the drug and implant companies, or the companies won't do it. For example, instead of injecting cancer cells into healthy animals to check that chemotherapy drugs are safe and work for human patients, we could study cancer in animals who are already sick and need treatment. We could discuss options fully with families and if they wanted their animal friend to be in a properly controlled study with the new and likely better drug, then we may help those animals to live longer, while also saving money for medicine and implant companies. In this way we could reduce and replace some of the animals currently needed for experimentation. Win-win!

I would love for my operations on animals to inspire human medicine, just as human medicine has inspired me. Every time I carry out an innovative surgery to solve a difficult problem, I write up the details of the procedure. I've published loads of scientific papers on new methods and my hope is that my work with animals inspires human doctors too. If vets and human surgeons work more closely together and share their knowledge, we can help animals and humans alike.

How We Are Different . . .
and How We Are the Same

All life on Earth – plant or animal – *evolved* from the same organism, which in turn evolved from the minerals of stardust many millions of years ago. Today, we humans share around 84% of our DNA with dogs, and almost 90% with cats. We all share the same basics: arms and legs, brains and skeletons, sensory organs to help us smell, see and hear, respiratory systems to help us breathe, cardiovascular organs to pump blood around our bodies and digestive tracts to turn food into energy and waste. The way bodies heal and how immune systems fight infection are the same.

Humans and Dogs

🐾 When together, the heart rates of dogs and humans slow down and potentially synchronise – talk about a connection!

- They might not have distinct paw prints like we have fingerprints, but did you know that every dog has their own unique nose print?

- Our skeletons have similar bones, but a dog has many more – over ten more teeth than humans, and up to twenty-three bones in their tails!

- Humans can sweat all over their bodies but a dog only has sweat glands on their paws and nose, and has to pant to cool down.

Humans and Cats

🐾 Cats have more bones (230) than humans (up to 213), but less than a dog (up to 321), and though a cat's spine has about thirty vertebrae, compared to a human's thirty-three, cat spines are more flexible, so they're able to squeeze into all sorts of odd places!

🐾 The primates which humans evolved from all had tails once, but now the only remaining sign of tails in humans is our coccyx (or tailbone), made of several vertebra that fused together at the bottom of our spine.

🐾 Cats, like dogs, have a much better sense of smell than we do, and they also have a wider field of vision, even if they don't see colours in the same way that we do.

🐾 Cats have an extra, semi-transparent eyelid that we don't have. It can protect their eyes when fighting other animals or moving through long grass.

CHAPTER 11
My Animal Family

Maybe it's because **my best friend growing up was a dog** or because I've known first-hand the unconditional love an animal shares, but I do not care for the word 'owners' to describe people who bring animals into their homes. I much prefer 'family' or 'human companions' or 'guardians'. I refer to those who bring their pets to the practice as 'mum' or 'dad'; if children come too, they're 'brothers' and 'sisters'.

I'm not trying to make animals more like humans, but rather trying to be more respectful to those we invite into our lives, and it's also much closer to how we see our animal friends. We don't own animals. We coexist with them. We share our sofas, our walks, our happy and sad moments. All of the cats and dogs who come through my doors are integral family members and are treated the same as if they were my personal friend – with respect and love. No matter how scared, hurt or anxious they may be, **I always believe that hugging is half of healing.**

From the earliest times in human history, when we evolved from tree-dwelling apes, we were part of the world. We belonged in the food chain, eating plants and other animals, but were prey for others. We should remember that with humility.

Once we learned how to harness fire, things changed. Now we could live more safely on the ground. We could cook our food, which meant it was easier to digest. We could roam further and gather in larger communities. Our brains grew more powerful and we learned to use animal furs and other materials to shield ourselves from the environment.

It's easy to think of us humans as being at the top of some sort of tree, isn't it? We take over the world wherever we step foot – using the earth's resources to make our lives easier. Often the animals that live in these places are an afterthought. I think that's completely wrong. We might be the cleverest in some ways, but that doesn't mean we're better, and it doesn't give us the right to use and abuse animals at will.

No one is sure exactly when we started to live closely with dogs or cats. But one thing is certain – we lived *alongside* them and the relationship was *reciprocal*. That means it benefitted both animal and person. **We have a special connection and I see it every day in my work.**

Dogs evolved from wolves – those that came closest to the fires of our ancestors to take scraps of food gradually became tamer. They helped us to herd and hunt other animals. They raised the alarm when other wild animals or strangers came close and threatened us. From those first tame wolves came the hundreds of breeds we see today. From tiny Chihuahuas to giant Great Danes, from the cuddliest Labrador to the fiercest looking German Shepherd. **We humans are responsible for all of the different types of dogs.** We bred them for different purposes – hunting, rescuing, guarding, catching rats, racing, etc. Sadly, sometimes we have also bred them with genetic problems which can cause big issues for their health. We need to take responsibility for this going forward. Pet dogs are more popular than ever before, and most people want an animal in their life for companionship more than any specific job the animal might do for them. **Dogs are amazing companions and bring joy to peoples' lives every day** across the world. Your dog is always

happy to see you come home – even if you've only been away for ten minutes. They really can make us better people and they believe in us. As the old saying goes, 'Be the person your dog thinks you are!'

Cats are more mysterious though. Unlike dogs, who tend to follow the patterns of their guardians, sleeping at night, cats are **'crepuscular'** – meaning they're most active at dawn or dusk, as I have said before. Humans have always feared big cats like tigers and lions – for good reason – but smaller wild cats lived closer to people for the same reason as dogs: they would get food! They in turn helped keep rodents and snakes away. **Cats are natural survivors and more solitary and self-reliant** – often happy to disappear for hours on end, hunting and exploring. Dogs are more sociable. In the wild, they live in packs and will normally welcome new animals into their household. Cats can be a lot more unpredictable – sulking for hours on end if their guardian gets a new pet or even letting their claws do the talking!

As kittens, they're normally sweet-natured, but as get older they can become less forgiving. They have more weapons at their disposal than dogs, they're incredibly agile and they aren't shy about letting you know they're cross. It's possibly more difficult to earn a cat's trust, I think. Treats don't work as well to get a cat on your side – they seem to know you're up to something!

I learned this through all the cats I've treated. Some will lay quietly in your lap and let you stroke their ears, others will cower in the back of a cage, arching their spines and hissing, lashing out with a lightning-fast paw armed with dagger-like claws.

Some say that the first human settlements adopted dogs and tamed them, whilst cats adopted humans and tamed them instead!

I should know, because two of my best friends are cats.

Excalibur and Ricochet

From the time of my boyhood friend, Pirate, I've always had animals in my life. I could not be without their companionship. As I write this book, **my companion Ricochet lays curled on my knee** in my messy office. Excalibur perches outside the window, on a specially constructed platform overlooking the fields beside the practice. They live with me wherever I go – whether that's my office and bedroom at the practice or whenever I get to go to my house. As I've mentioned, Ricochet is a dark black chocolate colour, with a fluffy mane of russet brown and huge bear-like paws. Excalibur is the same size as Ricochet and silver-tabby coloured. They are both Maine Coon cats, which is one of the oldest natural breeds of cat from North America. **They are gentle giants** and I love then more than I can put into words.

Both of them are incredible. They wait by the door when they hear me approaching and greet me with loud purring as soon as I walk in the room. They both love to curl up on my knee when I'm writing at my desk – Ricochet always climbs up from the left side and Excalibur from the right – and they're very respectful so if one is on my knee, the other just lies by my feet and vice versa.

Ricochet is hugely perceptive and sensitive. He knows when I am upset or feeling down and when I'm happy. He climbs up on my knee, purring like a buzzing engine, flings his arms up around my neck, pulls my face down to his and rubs his face and nose against mine several times a day. **He keeps checking in to make sure I'm OK.** His love is a luminescent beacon of joy in my life and I love him so much that my heart seems to swell with light whenever I see him.

Excalibur loves to be 'smooched', which is where I **nuzzle his fur and tickle him** all over. He always smells of fresh cotton. He is more independent that Ricochet and goes off to play with leaves in the garden, which he then brings back and hides in my bed. However, jumping into a bed of leaves isn't nearly so bad as jumping into my bed when he has hidden a screw or a piece of wire he's found in my office and it sticks in my bum! Until I covered up the model skeleton in my office, I found bits of rib bones or toes in my bed too. In many ways he and I are similar, in that when we get an idea in our head, we don't stop until we've fulfilled it. He just sits on the end of the bed and seems to smile, as if he knows exactly the prank he's played.

Also, there's nothing quite as sobering as being really tired, going to bed late at night and pushing earplugs into your ear, accompanied by the slow realisation that there is cat saliva running down your face, because he has found the ear plugs and chewed them during the day. And again, he smiles.

Both Ricochet and Excalibur have harnesses so that I can carry them anywhere with me or we can go for walks in unfamiliar places. It takes a little longer to tie my shoelaces, because they each tug at the ends, but this starts off the day with a smile. If I close my eyes for a nap on the bed in the room next to my office, they'll bop me on the head with a paw until I give them attention. And no matter how much water I put in their bowl, they still prefer to drink from my glass or mug.

They bring smiles throughout the day and the day ends with a smile too, as they climb up on my bed for night-time cuddles. I am so very lucky to have their love in my life, and I don't ever take a second of it for granted.

Keira

I try my best not to become too emotionally involved with the animals who come into the practice, but I do think that we should be more open about the role that love plays in our lives as medical practitioners. After all, that's why we signed up in the first place. Because of what I do,

I often see companion animals who are suffering. And their guardians are in pain too, heartbroken for their loved ones. When they're in my consulting room, the crisis of their animal friend often prompts people to share lots of the problems in their lives. Though I will only ever do what is in the animal's best interest, I think of both the animal and their human companion as being in my care. As well as a vet, I'm a shoulder to cry on and someone to talk to when times are tough.

Sometimes there's nothing I can do to make an animal better and I advise euthanasia. In such sad circumstances, it's really important that families have the peace of mind of knowing that they have done their very best for their very best friend. There's nothing quite like going through this with your own dearly beloved companion, though. I know it well, because I shared many ups and downs with my best friend ever in the whole wide world. Her name was

Keira and she was a gorgeous Border Terrier with a spikey-haired face and the most brilliant doggy smile I have ever seen.

A dog lives, on average, around twelve to fourteen years. That means that most people, if they get a dog as a puppy, will see his or her full life-span. From the playful furniture-chewing years when he or she is tugging on their lead, to the time when you don't need a lead at all and the old boy or girl is plodding along at your heels. I believe it's our responsibility to show that dog love from the first moment to the last, just as they love us. That's unconditional love, **the most precious gift in the world**. Maybe one of the reasons that your dog is always happy to see you is that their life passes on average seven times faster than ours and so every day for them could be considered a week for you or me. Maybe they realise that they need to cram as much love, light and joy as possible into each and every day.

I'd wanted a canine companion for a long time, but my life was complicated. Often, I was working sixteen or eighteen hours a day, so I knew I wouldn't have enough time for twice-daily walks and the affection and attention a puppy needs every

single day. Luckily, a nurse who worked with me, Amy, wanted a dog too, so we agreed to care for one together. Amy had a son called Kyle and together we became Keira's family.

Keira came into our lives as a twelve-week-old puppy, and **it was love at first sight** as she jumped into my arms. From then on, Keira split her life between the house where Amy and her son lived, the practice where I worked and often slept, and my house where I could occasionally go and cuddle up with her for a nice long sleep. Her bed was always beside mine, with one of my old T-shirts or sweaters that she could nestle into when I was taking care of other animals.

Keira was a common sight to those who work at Fitzpatrick Referrals, trotting along at my heels and sitting on my feet in my office, snoring softly as I wrote up surgical reports, studied for exams or wrote academic papers or books. She was a very patient dog, rarely barking or making mischief. She was always ready for a walk and wagged her rump furiously whenever I picked up her lead. For years, she went on my jogging runs with me. **If I was down, she knew how to lift me up** and her wise gaze kept me steady. Her love was the one constant and stable thing in my life throughout her life.

When she grew older, she developed cataracts (cloudy patches on the lens of the eye) and her hearing started to get worse too. Now I'd be first to rise in the morning, and I would wake her from her basket by gently laying a hand on her fur. She'd blink awake and roll over for a belly rub, then spring into life. When Ricochet and then Excalibur arrived, she welcomed them into the family immediately. She and Ricochet often curled up and slept together in her bed. It was very funny if Ricochet got there first, because Keira was so polite. Even though it was her bed, she would just nuzzle Ricochet to move over and slide in beside him.

When she was thirteen, disaster struck. I was leaving the practice one evening and, as we always did, I held open the door for Keira to trot out to my car. In the exact same moment, a van came into the car park, driving too fast. I didn't see it coming in time. Keira was small and it was dark. The driver couldn't have known that in that instant a little dog was ambling right into his path.

I screamed for him to stop, which made Keira freeze too. I reached for her, but it was too late.

I'll never forget the sound as the wheel of the van hit her and she yelped in pain. What followed is a blur. I was crying. I was *terrified*. I picked up Keira and cradled her broken body in my arms. In her confusion, she bit me for the first time ever. I didn't care. My colleagues at the practice came running and I'll be forever grateful for their calm that day as they organised themselves around me, because I couldn't have managed alone. Keira was rushed inside and stabilised with pain medication and a drip. We then took X-ray images and a CT scan. We didn't need to fully anaesthetise her – she was too badly hurt to do anything but remain still.

A hundred confused thoughts were fighting in my brain. **What were her injuries? Would she live, let alone walk again?** I was in shock. The X-ray images revealed a smashed jigsaw of broken and dislocated bones in her rear end, with damage to her pelvis, lower back and hip joint. But broken bones were the least of her worries. They could be mended. What concerned us more was the internal bleeding and organ damage. Either could cause a quick death. Overnight my colleagues constantly monitored her vital signs.

I was sent home – in no fit state to help – but my team would call if there was any news. I went, in a daze, and lay cuddling Ricochet, unable to sleep. In the morning, Keira was still critical whilst I was sent to the hospital to have my own bite wound treated. Once there, I was called to return to the practice as soon as possible. I knew what that meant, because I'd said the same to guardians when their own animal friends were close to death. It maybe meant a last goodbye.

Keira was struggling to breathe when I saw her. We weren't sure exactly what was happening inside her, so we rushed her across to another hospital which I used to own that dealt with soft tissue problems. A new CT scan revealed extensive and life-threatening damage to her bladder and belly lining. Tears in this lining, which is called the 'peritoneum', were leaking blood and her bladder was leaking urine, making toxic poisoning likely. She was dying quickly and we had to act fast.

My area of surgical expertise is bones, muscle and spine, so I handed over to my specialist soft tissue surgery colleagues and I shall also be forever grateful to them. The team saved her life that day. Her recovery would be long and hard, but I knew she was a fighter. She had a chance. When she woke, I was the first face she saw. She licked me, as if to say, 'Oh, there you are, Dada,' and I stroked her head until her eyes closed again.

It was just over a week later – seven days of worry and constant monitoring – that I gathered a team to deal with the other problems Keira had suffered. Though eating had been hard for her, she had gained enough physical strength to withstand the next operation – and this was one I'd need to perform myself. So that she could walk again without pain, I aimed to fix her many pelvic fractures, the damage to the sacrum of her lower spine and her dislocated hip joint. I needed to be strong enough mentally for what would be a tough surgery – this time on my very best friend in the whole world.

Based on her CT scan, my talented engineering colleague Jay had designed and built a custom metal plate to fit her particular fracture type and other screws and ligament implants would also be used. I had a plan of where to drill into her bones, but when I cut into her with the scalpel, I found the tissue damage was far worse than I had expected. Her bones were splintered with so many tiny cracks that even the detailed CT scan hadn't picked them all up. An operation that should have taken three hours took more like eight. By the end I was exhausted and lay beside her bed in the recovery ward. Keira's future was still uncertain, but we'd done all we could.

When she came round from the operation, she

was groggy from the anaesthesia, but there was hope in her eyes and she licked my face. In a few days she could bear her own weight. We had to be careful she didn't fuss at her stitches or do too much, and infection was an ever-present danger.

The tenacity of my patients never ceases to astonish me. Without complaint, they just get on with life. Keira's recovery was astonishing as hair grew back over her rear end, and her appetite returned. In a week she was walking, and in a month she was able to potter around again. We played 'the pea game' which is where she walked slowly along the corridor, getting stronger with each step and picking up one pea after another that was laid out like a trail of sweeties in front of her. She was slower than before but that didn't matter – I felt blessed every time I looked at her little spikey-haired face.

Keira lived another year after the operation and I am incredibly thankful for those extra months we shared. In

the end, old age took her, and she had a heart attack –
but it still hit me harder than any other moment in my
life. For all her fourteen years on this planet, she was my
confidante – a patient listener with whom I could share
anything. She went through all of life's ups and downs
with me and showed me nothing but unconditional
love for her entire life. I would not have been strong
enough to build my practice, Fitzpatrick Referrals,
without her constant companionship. I would not have
been brave enough to face each difficulty along the
way without her smiling face of encouragement. And
I would not have been good enough to study for loads
of exams and develop the inventions you've read about
in this book without her ever-knowing wisdom by my
side. I owe all of this to her inspiration and guiding light
and I wouldn't be the man I am even now without her
in my heart.

She was a spikey-haired, beard-snuffling, tear-licking,
crumb-hunting, foot-warming, bum-waggling bundle
of joy. She was, quite simply, the love of my life

and the greatest superpet I have ever known. 'Super', not because she was bionic, but because she had the kindest heart you could ever imagine, and I was so incredibly blessed that she shared it with me. Her superpower was invisible and immeasurable, but greater than any operation I can ever perform or any comic-book hero that ever inspired me. It was the superpower of *unconditional love*, which allowed me to be the very best I could be. And it was this very superpower that inspired everything you have just read.

Thank you, Keira.

I love you beyond time and space.

Unconditionally.

A FINAL MESSAGE
Not the End

We can learn a huge amount from animals, if we are open to them teaching us. I have learned daily from my animal family at home, at my practice and in the world throughout all of my life. I've seen thousands of poorly animals, big and small, and I am constantly amazed by their will to survive and their ability to give love and to accept ours. **Every cat and dog I meet has their own amazing story, as has their loving family.**

We humans, with our big brains, worry about a lot of things. Money, fame, failure and success, what we said to someone and what they said to us. Our animals companions aren't like that. Give them shelter and food and affection, and they're happy. Even when they've been through great pain, their eyes light up and their tails wag at the sight of their human companions.

In my job as an animal surgeon, I see the potential for treating our own medical problems if we can create a more caring world. I see a future where we respect the animals of our planet as much as our fellow person. It may sometimes be as challenging to earn an animal's trust and love as it is for a human, but once we have it, we should cherish it – forever. Love is so powerful – it can change not just your life, but the whole world. And the good news is, it's infinite. It won't run out. We just need to find it, harness it and spread it further.

So if you have an animal companion in your life, be thankful and be loving. Go and give them a cuddle. Suddenly the whole world will seem a better place to be.

GLOSSARY

AMPUTATION: an operation where a limb is removed.

ANAESTHETIC: a medicine that stops voluntary nerve signals travelling from the brain to the body or the body to the brain. It can be a 'local' injection which means it targets a certain area only locally and so the patient stays awake. Or it can be a 'general' anaesthetic where the animal is made completely unconscious.

BACTERIA: micro-organisms that cause infection.

BENIGN TUMOUR: a growth that is not cancerous and doesn't spread to other areas of the body.

BIONIC SURGERY: this is where a body part is replaced with a man-made (artificial) implant which aims to provide a similar function to the original part.

BIRTH CANAL: the area of the body that babies come out of.

BLOOD VESSELS: the tubes that ferry blood around the body.

BONE MARROW: soft, spongy insides of some bones where stem cells come from, producing all kinds of tissue, from blood cells to cells that connect the body parts together, known as connective tissue.

CALCANEUS: the large bone forming the heel.

CARDIOVASCULAR SYSTEM: where blood travels through the body, including the heart and blood vessels.

CARPUS: wrist bones.

CARTILAGE: strong, flexible connective tissue that lines the ends of bones or from which bones grow. 'Articular' cartilage allows bones to

glide smoothly against each other
inside joints, whilst 'growth plates'
made from cartilage near the ends
of many bones (the medical term
is 'physes') converts into bone as
young animals and children grow. This
'physeal' cartilage allows us all to
'grow up', quite literally.

CREPUSCULAR: the term for animals
that are most active at dawn or
dusk.

CT (COMPUTED TOMOGRAPHY) SCAN:
an image of an area of a body made
up of many X-ray images combined
using a computer, creating a three-
dimensional 'density map' of any body
part.

DEGENERATIVE HEALTH PROBLEM: when an illness gets worse over time.

DEHYDRATION: lack of water.

DNA: the genetic information code inside the nucleus or centre part of any of the body's cells.

DRIP: a plastic tube with a needle on one end and a bag on the other, which is inserted into a vein, so that fluids and medicines can travel directly into the bloodstream from the bag.

ENDOPROSTHESIS: a prosthesis (artificial part) inside the body ('endo' means 'inside').

ENDOSCOPE: a surgical tool that consists of a long, flexible tube with a light at one end and a camera at the other to look inside the body.

ETHICS: what it means to do the right thing for yourself and others.

EUTHANASIA: when a patient is allowed to pass away peacefully with the help of medication.

EXOPROSTHESIS: a prosthesis (artificial part) outside the body ('exo' means 'outside').

EXTERNAL SKELETAL FIXATOR (ESF): a metal scaffold or frame on the outside of a limb to hold bone pieces

in place using pins or wires that pass through the skin into the bone and are attached to the frame on the outside using clamps.

FEMUR: the thigh bone.

FORCEPS: an instrument with two long, narrow arms for holding things.

GANGRENE: this condition occurs when the blood supply can't reach an area of tissue and it dies.

HUMANE: to treat others with kindness.

IMPLANT: any kind of artificial tissue or device such as a metal plate or screws, or an electrical conducting wire (electrode), for example,

which is put inside the body of
an animal or person.

INFLAMMATION: a process where the
immune system of the body reacts to
injury or fights infections like bacteria
and viruses, or when things like pollen
or chemicals trigger an unpleasant, but
necessary, reaction in the body. When
the inflammation comes from injuries
and infections, it often presents as
heat, redness, pain and swelling.

INTESTINE: 'guts' inside an animal or
human, where food is digested.

MALIGNANT TUMOUR: a growth
that is cancerous, which is a disease
where some of the body's cells grow
uncontrollably, attacking tissues such

as bones, skin, internal organs or glands, and usually spreading to other parts of the body.

METACARPAL BONES: palm bones.

METACARPO-PHALANGEAL JOINTS: knuckle joints of the front paws of many animals, including cats and dogs.

METATARSUS: the bones that make up the arch of the hind foot of a dog or cat.

NEURO-ORTHOPAEDIC SURGERY: cutting open and operating on patients to fix problems associated with the skeleton, joints, muscles, tendons, spine and nerves.

NEUTERING: surgical removal of reproductive organs.

OESOPHAGUS: the pipe that carries food from the mouth to the stomach.

OSTEOARTHRITIS: inflammation of all the tissues that make up a joint, which includes the fluid, the sac that holds the fluid, the cartilage, the bone underneath and around the cartilage and the ligaments and support structures around the joint.

PELVIS: the rectangular bone structure that connects the spine to the hind legs.

PERITONITIS: inflammation or

infection of the inner lining of the tummy, which is medically called the 'abdomen' and holds many organs like the liver, kidneys and intestines (guts).

PESTICIDES ('PEST-KILLERS'): a substance used to kill or repel forms of animal or plant life, such as insects and fungi, that are considered a nuisance in agriculture or in the life of humans or larger animals.

PLATELETS: tiny disc-shaped pieces of very large cells, derived from bone marrow cells that are released into the bloodstream. These help form clots to stop bleeding as well as carrying very important chemical

signals to help with healing and other functions in the body.

PROSTHESES: artificial body parts.

PUS: a thick yellow or green oozing liquid from a wound that has become infected. Pus consists of dead white blood cells, bacteria, cells discarded by the body and serum — the fluid in which blood cells flow around the body.

RADIUS: one of the bones that make up the forearm of a human, which is at the front of a cat or dog's front leg below the elbow (in front of the ulna bone), since the front legs of a dog or cat are equivalent to the arms of a human.

STETHOSCOPE: an instrument for listening to a heartbeat.

TALUS: one of the large bones that make up the ankle joint. It articulates (moves against) the shin bone or tibia.

THERMOMETER: an instrument for measuring temperature.

TIBIA: the shin bone of the lower leg below the knee joint.

TITANIUM: a silver-grey metal that is very strong and resists corrosion, which is used in the manufacture of many types of implants because of its compatibility with tissue and bone cells.

ULNA: one of the bones that make up the forearm of a human, which is at the back of a cat or dog's front leg below the elbow (behind the radius bone), since the front legs of a dog or cat are equivalent to the arms of a human.

URINARY BLADDER: the organ that holds urine (pee), which is like a balloon that inflates with fluid processed and excreted by the kidneys through two pipes. When the bladder is full, it tells the animal (or human) through nerve feedback that they need to empty this balloon through another pipe to the outside, getting rid of the fluid the body doesn't need after drinking and eating.

VERTEBRAE: the bones that form the spine (often referred to as the 'back bone', but in fact is composed of many smaller bones). They are like train carriages, one after the other, and the buffer between each carriage is an intervertebral disc. The disc is like a jam doughnut with a gel-like centre and a doughy outside, absorbing forces and allowing the spinal column to move in any direction.

WINDPIPE: the airway pipe that carries air in and out of lungs. The medical name for the windpipe is the trachea.

WOBBLER DISEASE: the name for a condition affecting the spine of

large and giant breed dogs. It's called
'wobbler' because these dogs wobble
due to an interruption in the nerve
signals passing through the neck
from the brain to the legs. Since
the back legs are furthest from this
disruption, the nerve impulses take
longer to travel, causing the dog to
wobble. The interruption of nerve
signals is caused by the spinal cord
in the neck being squashed either
by bulging intervertebral discs (if a
disc is compared to a jam doughnut,
the dough bulges because the disc
dries out) or by abnormally shaped
vertebrae squashing the spinal cord
with bone ('osseous tissue' is the
medical term). The technical name
for this condition is therefore
either 'Disc-Associated Wobbler

Syndrome' (DAWS for short)
or 'Osseous-Associated Wobbler
Syndrome' (OAWS for short).

X-RAY: an image created from
X-ray beams generated in a machine,
which pass through the body and
are received by a film or digital
receiver that converts the beams as
they come out the other side into
a 'density map' of that body part.
This is viewed in black and white on
what is commonly called an 'X-ray',
but should more correctly be called
an 'X-ray image' or a radiograph.
For example, bone appears white
because very few X-ray beams get
through, whereas the lungs are black
because they're full of air and many
X-ray beams get through.